A financial book that offers the i
near demise and revival of a community bank.

In existence since 1832, the Wilmington Savings Fund Society, a Delaware bank, teetered on the brink of closure in 1991. Written by former bank CEO Schoenhals, in collaboration with Kriegstein, this book traces the bank's journey from before its near-death experience through its successful rebirth…Schoenhals writes in the preface that the book's "one primary purpose" is for "past, current and future WSFS Associates and Customers" to gain a better understanding of the bank's history. In that respect, the story is largely a memoir by Schoenhals and other officials quoted in the volume. But this well-told tale has broader implications; intertwined with the WSFS chronicle are historical details about a previously precarious economic time, insights into actions taken by federal regulators, and glimpses of how banks are capitalized.

The work begins with a short, illustrated history of the bank, including an intriguing piece of trivia: In 1972, WSFS introduced what "was believed to be the world's first debit card." A chapter then offers a historical perspective on why the period from 1979 to 1990 was a particularly challenging time for financial institutions. Subsequent chapters explain in detail how WSFS got into serious trouble and was ultimately bailed out by investors. But this is not a dull, dry story; the lively account features sketches of bank, regulator, and investor personalities; the personal ups and downs faced by Schoenhals; a bailout plan written down on the proverbial napkin; and an amusing scene of a crucial slide presentation projected onto a bedsheet because no screen was available. Appended to the book is a section by Schoenhals of "stories that should not be lost." In this insightful retrospective, he shares perhaps some of his most valuable observations about the bank's culture, the "regulatory courage" it took to keep WSFS alive, and his seasoned views of leadership. ~*Kirkus Reviews*

Cover and Text Design by Strunk Creative

Printed and Bound by Cann Printing

From Failing to Phenomenal

The Story of WSFS
1985 to 1996

By Marvin 'Skip' Schoenhals

With Brittany Kriegstein

TABLE OF CONTENTS

About This Book

This book is a mix of voices and narrations, the result of a collaborative effort between Marvin 'Skip' Schoenhals and Brittany Kriegstein with additional reporting by Dan Tipton. Skip became president and CEO of WSFS on November 1, 1990, and the title of chairman was added in 1992. In 2007, Mark Turner became president and CEO, and in 2017 Skip retired as chairman, continuing as a director until 2021. Brittany is a journalist and writer based in New York City, and Dan is a communications consultant.

While the official writing of this book began in the winter of 2020, the idea for a memoir of WSFS began as conversations between Peggy Eddens, then executive vice president, Mark, and Skip in 2007. Though Mark had officially taken over the role of CEO, Skip remained very much a presence within the WSFS halls— as non-executive chairman, with an office on the bank's main floor. But Skip had also taken on another responsibility: Chief Storyteller. New Associates and friends alike would assemble in the lobby and at luncheons to hear him recount the trials and tribulations of the bank's rise from the ashes.

As the story was repeated time and again, Peggy, Skip and Mark realized that it needed to be preserved for posterity. What would happen when Skip and his contemporaries were no longer able to share those details? Added encouragement came in 2016, when Dominic Canuso was hired as WSFS chief financial officer. At a breakfast meeting with Skip sharing some of the history, he remarked that he'd tried to research the bank's history, but couldn't find anything. How could an institution with such a colorful past have no written chronicle to show for it? Along the way several WSFS directors, especially those new to the company, and particularly, Karen Buchholz, expressed enthusiasm for the project.

A few years prior, the WSFS team had enlisted the help of Dan Tipton to capture as much of the bank's history as he could by interviewing the key players who had lived through it. However, the interviews had never been woven into the complete story. So in 2020, Skip and Brittany Kriegstein wove those interviews— along with historical accounts, documents, newspaper articles and photographs— into the larger narrative we have today. Their collective work has ensured that the WSFS story will forever remain part of our DNA, inspiring generations of friends and Associates to come.

Part of the journey chronicled in this book is told by the headlines and stories about WSFS that were in the (Wilmington) News Journal. To give the reader a feel for this part of the journey, we have included reproductions of some of the more interesting articles. Unfortunately, due to physical size constraints of the book and quality of some of the archives, the print in some of the articles is difficult to read. In those cases where we deemed it important to be able to easily read the article, it has been reproduced in the Appendix. In the other cases, the headlines give sufficient color to the story.

Preface to Book 1— By Skip Schoenhals

This book covers the story of WSFS from the mid-1980s through early 1996. Looking at WSFS in late 2021 (when this book was finished), it's an exceptional company: We have nearly 2,000 Associates working in 111 offices across five states, and have been rated one of the best places to work in Delaware— now Philadelphia as well— for multiple years. Accolades include being named to the Forbes 'Best Banks' list in 2021 and the Bank Director's 2021 'RankingBanking' list, where WSFS' fourth-place spot categorizes it as a financial institution that has "built enviable value" for its shareholders over a 20-year period.

"Enviable value" is right. Anyone who has owned WSFS stock from the early 1990s to 2021 has enjoyed a return of 1859%. For comparison's sake, the S&P 500 Index produced a return of only 515% during the same period. On the human side of things, our Associates' unwavering dedication to the communities we serve, especially over the last three decades, helped build a company so entrenched in their customers' lives that they often say with gusto that they simply can't imagine a world without WSFS.

Indeed, for many looking at WSFS today, it doesn't seem remotely possible that in 1991, the bank was within inches of **being closed forever.**

In its early days, WSFS was a fairly conservative Savings and Loan (often called a "thrift" as well). Through the Civil War, both World Wars, and the Great Depression, the bank's humble reliability made it a stable life raft for its clients— safeguarding their finances in the face of great hardships. After the economic crash of 1929, for example, millions of people were left to watch helplessly as their savings disappeared when more than 9,000 banks were forced to permanently close. Against all odds, WSFS soldiered on through the storm, helping to keep its customers afloat and their funds intact.

But times change. The 1970s and 1980s were an era of significant shifts in the financial markets— with drastic impact on banks and thrifts in particular. From 1986 to 1995, more than 1,000 savings and loan associations failed— about a third of the thrifts that had existed in the United States up until that point.* Thankfully, the FDIC had come into being in 1933, so very few retail customers lost their savings, but many communities were hurt by the loss of local financial institutions— both because of the jobs they had created, and the businesses they had helped succeed.

This time around, WSFS was not immune to the misfortune that befell many of its peers. After celebrating its 150th birthday in 1982, the Wilmington thrift began to see its own health decline— due to forces both internal and external. The bank would continue on a rocky road through the beginning of the 1990s, spending more than three years on "life support."

This book tells the story of those turbulent decades— an exciting and terrifying account of the early 80s to the late 90s. It is a story of commerce and culture; of perseverance and grit. It is written with one primary purpose: To give past, current and future WSFS Associates and Customers an understanding of where we have come from, and for you all to realize that you are (or were) a crucial part of sustaining and continuously improving a truly great institution.

Only a handful of public companies have been in existence for almost two centuries, and we are one of them. As we celebrate nearly two hundred years of WSFS, it's difficult to believe that we were once "the sixth bank in a five-bank market"— low on morale and wondering if the world might move on without us. Yet, WSFS stood tall throughout the Global Financial Crisis of 2007-2008 and the disruption wrought by the Coronavirus pandemic. Now, we are the leading independent bank in the Delaware, Philadelphia and Southeast Pennsylvania market.

In the introduction that follows, we begin to explain how perilously close WSFS came to ending a nearly two-century run. The first chapter will step back in time, providing a brief flyover of the company's first century and a half. Chapter two looks at the economic events of the 1970s and 80s that led up to the "Thrift Crisis" of the 1990s, which ultimately engulfed WSFS. Chapters three through ten detail the company's nail-biting riches-to-rags-to-riches journey from 1985-1996, laying the foundation for the bank's entry into the 21st century. This is followed by some reflections from Skip entitled a 'Speck of Dust'.

Book Two, being written now by Mark Turner, will pick up the story from 1996 to his retirement as CEO in 2019: A career of building on the stability achieved in the late '90s, thereby turning WSFS into the dynamic and esteemed institution that it is today. Every present and future Associate will continue to be the creators of the ongoing legacy of the Wilmington Savings Fund Society.

* Curry, T., & Shibut, L. (2000). The Cost of the Savings and Loan Crisis. FDIC Banking Review, 13(2), 26-35.

Introduction
"The Keys, Please."

The weather on June 19, 1991, should have been an indication: The temperature— just 65 degrees— felt ominously cold for a late spring morning in Delaware, and the gray skies were a sign that more than an inch of rain would fall on Wilmington before the day was done. Marvin 'Skip' Schoenhals didn't know it yet, but dark, heavy clouds were also forming inside the WSFS boardroom. He was about to walk into the most emotional business meeting of his life. The 44-year-old banker had become president and CEO of WSFS eight months before, and while the beloved Delaware institution had seen better days, he and the other leaders felt that the rough patch it was going through would not be a death sentence.

"I'd gone into this meeting naively thinking, 'All right, we're okay. They're just here to give us the results of the exam,'" Skip remembers. Even though the bank had been through significant challenges in the previous few months, Skip had been working closely with a particular bank regulator who told him not to worry: The meeting would just be a routine presentation of the results of a recent examination of the bank's financial health.

But, as more than a dozen federal bank regulators filed somberly into the WSFS boardroom— outnumbering the WSFS board members— it quickly became clear that this day would be anything but ordinary. Especially foreboding was the fact that both the regional director of the FDIC and the regional director of the OTS were in attendance— a rare occurrence.[1]

The meeting started and the regulators began to speak, one by one. As each of them touched on a different part of the exam, the tension in the room increased dramatically. Every regulator painted a bleak picture of a bank with no hope for survival.

"In essence, each one of them said in their own words, 'We've examined the bank, things are really bad. We don't see how you are going to make it,'" recalls Skip.

How bad was it? A bank of WSFS' size was required to have $75 million in capital (the net worth of a bank); WSFS only had $5 million.

The money had evaporated with terrifying speed. At the start of 1990, WSFS had boasted a healthy $90 million in capital. However, by December 31 of 1990, the consequences of decisions made over the previous few years converged with a collapse in real estate values, causing $85 million of that capital to disappear. In those 12 months, the bank went from meeting all capital requirements (i.e. no serious regulatory concerns) to being dead in the center of the metaphorical regulatory radar screen focused on troubled financial institutions.

Now, the regulators made it clear that WSFS was out of time. Their recommendation: Shutter the bank and sell the healthy parts of the then 159-year-old thrift. Without further ado, they asked the bank's directors to sign a document that would give them approval to "shop the bank"— thereby bestowing upon them the additional authority they needed to sell the "good parts" of WSFS to another institution as they closed the bank forever.

"They said basically, 'give us the keys right now. We're here to take over.' Yeah, it came out of the blue," recalls CG Cheleden, WSFS board chairman at the time. "They were ready that day to take over the bank."

Mind racing as the fateful meeting progressed, Skip saw his whole career flash before his eyes. He'd been hired as CEO just eight months before to lead the effort to bring WSFS back to health. It was gut-wrenching to think that WSFS, a revered community bank with more than a century and a half of history, could come to such a devastating end under his watch.

"I'm sitting there as each guy speaks, frankly getting more and more depressed," Skip remembers. "I've relocated my family. I'm hearing, 'it's all over.' I'm not going to be given a chance. They're telling me they're going to take over, close the bank, sell it, and I'd be out of a job."

On a deeply personal level, Skip had just come through a three-year period of career instability: He had been fired twice, and had "sold himself out" of a third job. In other words, he had been out of work on three separate occasions; understandably, the prospect of another such episode was profoundly troubling. "I think pure panic would be the right choice of words to describe my feelings at that moment," he recalls.[2]

But in the pits of that dread, something clicked. Skip decided that he was not going down without a fight. Determined to alter the regulators' path, he delivered an impromptu speech over the next 40 minutes, hoping to sway them to give WSFS more time to strengthen its position. It was an impassioned plea, backed by a solid plan: With an extended lifeline, WSFS had a future.

When Skip was finished, CG stepped in with tangible proof that the WSFS team was working to improve the situation. Over the previous several months, the two leaders had been successful in obtaining some non-binding commitment letters from potential investors who would help to recapitalize the bank.

"We got out the [investor presentation] books and handed them around," CG remembers. "I said, 'Here we are. We're on the verge of raising capital. What are you doing?'"

Books and letters in hand, the two regional directors looked at each other and said, "Let's adjourn for a few minutes. Let's go and talk about it."

Everyone left the boardroom. The clock ticked forward, with the fate of WSFS hanging in the balance. It felt like an eternity.

After about half an hour had passed, Skip came walking back from his office, down the hallway towards the board room. He came across the two regional directors standing just outside.

"Skip, we're not quite sure what to do," one of them said. "You made a compelling case."

Sensing a fleeting opportunity, Skip thought on his feet. "Why don't you let me come to Washington to make my case?"

Washington, of course, was where the FDIC and OTS were headquartered. Skip was asking to make a direct appeal to the bosses of the two regional directors— his second Hail Mary attempt in this saga.

In a stroke of luck, or perhaps wisdom, the two regulators looked at each other and nodded their heads in unison. They gave Skip the green light to make the trip. "That gave us a lease on life in that they agreed to let us come to Washington; at least they weren't going to shut us down during that period of time," Skip said.

While the June meeting ended with a small sigh of relief from Skip, CG, and the other WSFS board members, they certainly were not yet out of the woods. The road ahead would be full of twists and turns, trials and tribulations, and each would question if WSFS truly had what it took to stand the test of time.

What follows here is the full story of that test, and the way in which WSFS rose to meet challenges beyond its founders' wildest dreams. Each brings to light the unique qualities of a team and a community that came together, surmounting life-threatening obstacles. Against all odds, WSFS not only survived— it flourished. The future, once an impossibility, ended up being bolder and brighter than anyone could have imagined.

[1] At the time WSFS's primary regulator was the Office of Thrift Supervision ('OTS'). The Federal Deposit Insurance Corporation ('FDIC') was considered the 'secondary' regulator. In normal circumstances, the FDIC would only be in the background and usually defer to the primary regulator. Rarely, if ever, would they show up at a board meeting. The OTC's functions (primarily supervising savings & loans) were transferred to the Comptroller of the Currency in 2011 and the OTS dissolved.

[2] This might lead the reader to ask, why in the world did WSFS hire Skip? The answer is that his career had been very successful up to that point. By age 40, he had become a senior officer in one of the most successful bank holding companies in Michigan. He had already led two troubled banks to calm waters, but one of those success stories led to him being sold out of a job. Skip reflects a bit more on the impact of losing his job in the section at the end of this book.

Chapter 1
A Look Back in Time—
The First 150 Years

Long before automobiles, airplanes and electricity, a well-respected Delaware judge named Willard Hall met with a group of prominent Wilmingtonians to talk about creating a place for the local townspeople to put their money.

It was **August 1831**. Andrew Jackson was vying for a second term as president. Religious texts were still more widely-read than secular books or newspapers. Fire had to be created by friction; there were no matches. Gas and coal power were still years away, and telephones, radios and television sets would not come about for decades. But the country was changing. Stagecoaches, still the most common mode of transportation, saw the birth of a newfangled challenger: railroads. Little by little, locomotive branches were extending into new American cities, creating an unprecedented web of connectivity between them that would usher in the dawn of a new era.

As the country spun towards innovation, Wilmington's 7,000 residents were already hard at work at the various mills that lined the banks of the Brandywine. They helped the budding city make a name for itself in the production of cotton, flour, paper, and especially gunpowder, as home to the burgeoning DuPont Company that would become a titanic force in American industry.[3]

The citizens' productivity, while admirable, was just the thing concerning Willard Hall and his peers: No place existed for the average person to safeguard his or her savings. Banks were scarce, and even fewer accepted the kinds of small deposits that Wilmingtonians brought home to hide under their mattresses, having no other options. Lots of money was lost or stolen as a result, and none of it earned interest. It was time to come up with a solution.

"It was considered, that an Institution that would encourage such savings by taking charge of them, and putting them into some secure way of accumulation, would not only benefit individuals in a pecuniary respect, but exert a very salutary moral influence— would be an unexceptionable and efficacious mode of benevolence."

So read a report from an 1831 meeting of Wilmington Savings Fund Society's Board of Managers, a 25-person committee that had been elected that September. On October 1, Willard Hall was made president. A man who had spent decades devoting himself to the cause of popular education, Hall was a natural choice to head the fledgling Savings Fund Society— a new educational project of sorts that would teach the average resident a thing or two about how to put savings away for a rainy day.

From the start, the individuals in charge of the Savings Fund agreed on a few fundamentals:

1. The new institution would not be operated for profit, except to its depositors.
2. There would be no stockholders.
3. Deposits were to be conservatively invested and used for only three purposes— to accumulate an adequate cash reserve for the depositors' protection; to pay interest on such deposits; and to meet all necessary expenses that would arise.

Therefore, the only purpose of the society was to encourage thrift. While the world— and banking— have certainly changed since then, that core tenet has stayed with WSFS for the last two centuries.

The Early Days (1832-1900)

On **February 18, 1832**, the Wilmington Savings Fund Society officially opened its doors for business. Its first "office" was a small rented room, below Town Hall. It was only open on Saturdays from 10 a.m. to noon, and then again from 2 p.m. to 4 p.m. Deposits had to be at least $1, but not more than $20, and interest was set at 3.6%.

Old Town Hall, built 1798. Drawing by Leon DeValinger.
Courtesy of the Delaware Historical Society.

For those of us living in the age of deposits and withdrawals done mostly on our Smartphones, it's hard to picture the fact that banking used to be somewhat of a cozy, family affair. At the very first headquarters of WSFS, the treasurer led operations— doing all the accounting from his post at the "banker's desk." He and his wife and children would have lived in the building, supplying heat, light and maintenance instead of paying rent. Other daily tasks would have included replenishing the sand used for blotting, and providing the potatoes into which goose quill pens were stuck.[4]

By **February of 1833**, one year after its founding, deposits in the Wilmington Savings Fund Society totaled $12,402. While that doesn't seem like very much by modern standards, it translates to more than $380,000 in today's dollars[5] — a clear sign that the idea of keeping money in the bank was catching on around town. What's more, a standard national currency hadn't yet been established, so much of the money being deposited were notes printed at private presses around the state.

The next several decades held a series of milestones for the young bank, including three different moves to larger buildings as deposits flowed in. In **1840**, the Wilmington Savings Fund Society adopted its official seal, and bought itself a new home at 611 Market Street for $4,750. By **1856**, it had outgrown that location, and had completed an ambitious project to build new headquarters on a vacant lot at the southeast corner of Eighth and Market Streets. "It became one of the showplaces of the city, its distinctive front being made of heavy sheets of iron," read a historical account of the site in the February 17th edition of *The Morning News*.

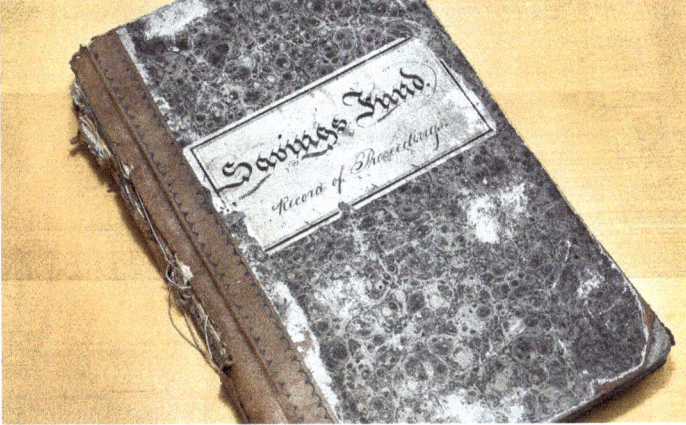

The First Minute Book of the Wilmington Savings Fund Society
Photo: Floyd Dean—Dean Digital Imaging

On **April 2, 1861**, the WSFS board secretary began to write in the bank's second minute book, filling it with the numbers and figures of a growing institution. Ten days afterwards, shots were fired on Fort Sumter, and the nation plunged into the Civil War. While that year would see the first decrease in deposits at the bank since its inception, WSFS held firm through the tumult. In **1862**, the bank invested $40,000 in United States Securities, demonstrating its faith in the Union and preserving Delaware as part of it. The bank also committed itself to donating money to sick and wounded soldiers, earmarking $1,000 for those brave men and their families at a meeting of the managers on **September 30, 1862**. When the Federal Government placed a tax on deposits, WSFS paid that tax for its customers "to preserve interest at 5% heretofore." Only at this point did President Lincoln pass the **National Banking Act of 1863**, unifying and regulating financial institutions and making standard, government-issued currency.

Despite the havoc wreaked by the bloody war and the initial chaos caused by the National Banking Act, WSFS continued to prosper. In **1866**, the bank recognized founder Willard Hall by commissioning his portrait— which still hangs in WSFS' Hall of Founders, along with every other president since that time. After 41 years of service, he resigned as the Society's President in **1872**.

"We shall sadly miss his wise counsel and courteous manners and find it almost impossible to obtain one to fill his place— his equal in all respects," read a testimonial to the elderly Judge Hall in board minutes from that year. He was succeeded by Joseph Bringhurst.

By the end of **1883**, deposits at WSFS breached the $1 million mark— undoubtedly an unthinkable watershed moment for the bank's founders just half a century earlier. With that milestone came the need for new headquarters once again. The Society purchased land on the corner of Ninth and Market Streets in **1885**, and set about constructing the kind of place that would proudly take WSFS into the future. When it opened in **1887**, the new building showcased many of the features that would become hallmarks of bank headquarters in decades to come: A spacious public lobby, executive offices at the back, tellers' cages, space for files, a large board room, and a modern vault. The treasurer, no longer a live-in resident, had his own office to the left of the main entrance.

Besides the interior's state-of-the-art features, WSFS' operations also shifted to accommodate a more modern lifestyle. The bank was now open from 9 a.m. to 3 p.m. daily, allowing customers to withdraw their money without prior notice for the first time. The only telltale sign that it was still the late 1800s: On the corner of the bank's property stood a small shed, used by the president to stable his horse during business hours.

A New Century of Saving

The turn of the 20th century marked the beginning of a new era for WSFS, where the bank thought up creative strategies to connect with members of the local community like never before. One example was its participation in the Penny Provident Initiative of **1900**, which encouraged local schoolchildren to start saving their pennies. An excerpt from the January 25 edition of the Delaware Gazette and State Journal detailed how students from the No. 15 School at Fourth and Harrison streets were involved:

"Of the 425 pupils in the school, about 100 are depositors in the fund. Of this number five have deposited more than $8, and Miss Elizabeth Carlisle, one of the teachers, who has charge of the matter, has transferred their money to the Wilmington Savings Fund Society, where accounts have been opened for them. They continue saving in the provident fund and their savings will be deposited from time to time in the Savings Fund to their credit. Up to the present time the children of the school have saved $104.41."

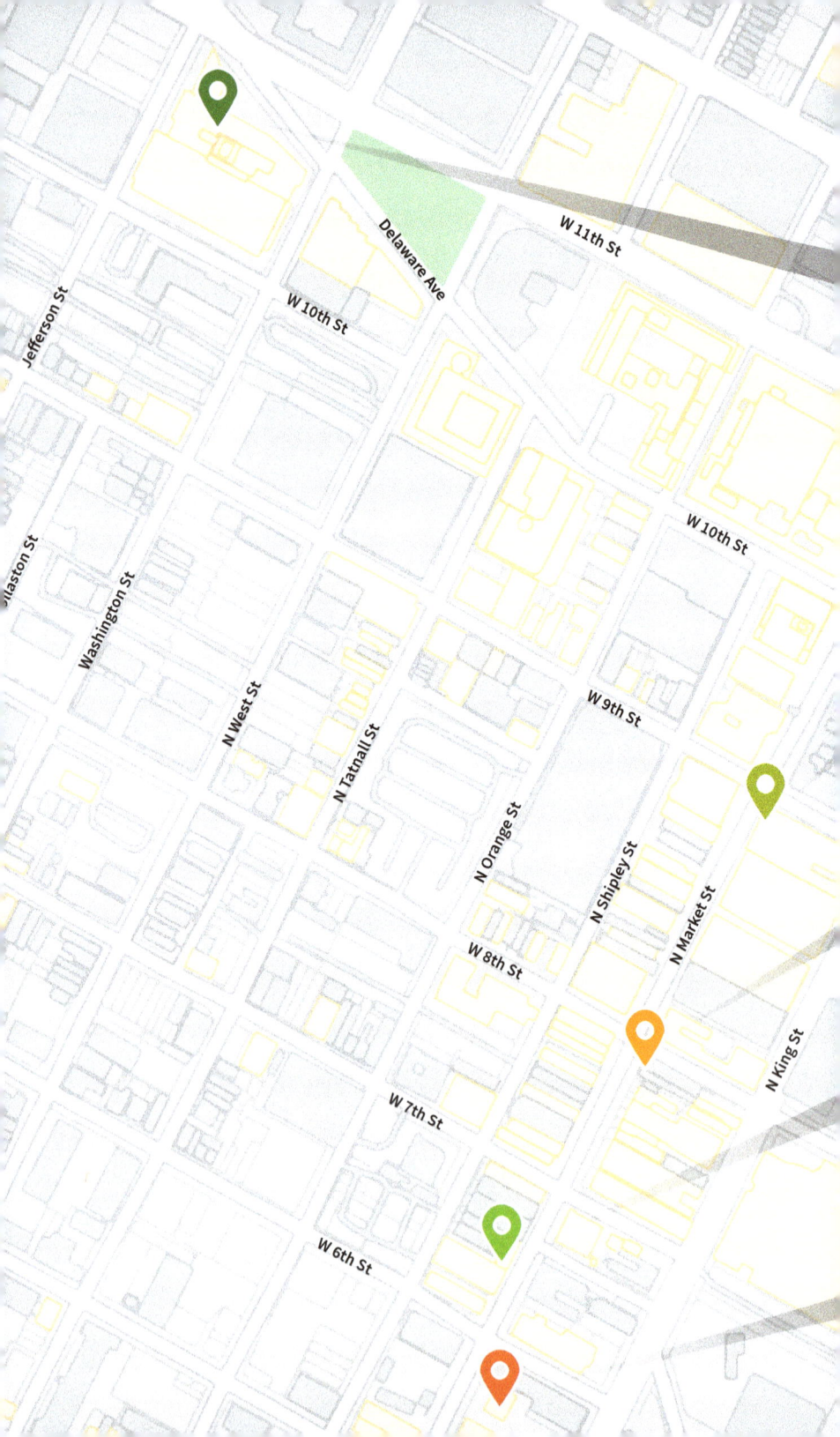

Locations over the years.

500 Delaware Avenue

9th and Market Street

8th and Market Street

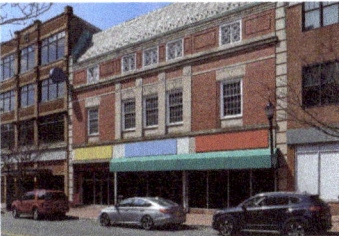

611 Market Street

500 block of Market Street

Ninth and Market Street building, constructed in 1885. WSFS archives.

The Gazette praised the project for giving young people the incentive to set aside money for the future— an important practice that would no doubt serve them well in their adult lives.

"Each depositor has a book and is given due credit for each deposit. The fact that they can save their pennies in that manner has a tendency to make them desire to swell their savings rather than spending the money as they get it."

In truth, it was increasingly prudent for WSFS to be engaging with prospective customers: Competition was expanding, with 18 new banks chartered across the state in the early part of the new century. Some of that had to do with a population boom, but staying relevant to the people of Delaware was more important than ever if the bank wanted to continue seeing positive results.

By **1920**, it was deemed time to advance with the times once again. Yet another new building was authorized for construction at WSFS' 9th and Market Street property— one that would contain "modern equipment," including the bank's first electrically-guarded vault. As always, keeping customers confident about the safety of their precious funds was first and foremost on the bank's list of priorities.[6]

Outside new building on Ninth and Market Street. *Courtesy of the Delaware Historical Society.*

Inside new building on Ninth and Market Street. *Courtesy of the Delaware Historical Society.*

By the time **1928** rolled around, the bank faced a need for extended facilities on the West Side of Wilmington. WSFS acquired property at Union and Third Streets and opened its first branch.[7]

Union Street Office at Third. WSFS archives.

But the faith that Wilmingtonians had in their local bank would be put to the ultimate test in **October of 1929**, when the stock market crashed. As news of economic distress spread across the county, panicked citizens rushed into community banks, demanding to withdraw their cash. The problem: Most banks had invested their money in various loans, and now didn't have the funds on-hand to give them back.

Not surprisingly, people lost trust in the very institutions that were supposed to come to the rescue when the going got tough. WSFS wasn't immune to the panic, as minutes from the Board of Managers meeting on **November 12th, 1929**, suggest:

"At the conclusion of the regular business, the President outlined the difficulties we were having, at this time, owing to the heavy withdrawals occasioned by many individuals drawing funds to protect margin accounts, making investments, and for fear occasioned by scare headlines in the Every Evening."

Even so, WSFS was not among those hardest hit— as many banks around the country were being temporarily shuttered or restricted by the government, the Delaware State Bank Commissioner reported at the time that "no Delaware bank closed during the period until the Bank Holiday."[8]

Back in 1929, there had been 17,583 state banks and 8,150 national banks in the U.S., according to historical data from the FDIC. From 1930 to 1933, about 4,000 U.S. banks and 1,700 Savings & Loans closed their doors for good— damaged beyond repair by the lingering depression. However, life at WSFS during that period looked markedly different. With nearly $20 million in deposits from over 35,000 depositors, in **1930**, the bank was preparing for its centennial anniversary. It spent $25,000 (more than $460,000 in today's dollars!) to commission an enormous mural by renowned local artist N.C. Wyeth to properly commemorate the occasion.

After two years of work, The Apotheosis of the Family was unveiled to the public at the bank's official centennial celebration on **February 18, 1932**. At first glance, it appeared to center around common

imagery: family, home, survival, the four seasons. But a closer analysis revealed how each bold scene highlighted industry, preservation, and, ultimately, thrift.

The Apotheosis of the Family.

Measuring a colossal 60 feet by 19.5 feet, Wyeth's epic painting—definitely the largest in Wilmington at the time, and among the grandest in the country— was mounted on a specially-designed wall of the WSFS headquarters lobby, where it would remind generations of future WSFS Associates and customers what the bank represented at its core.[9]

"There are not many savings banks in the United States that are 100 years old," read an article in the morning edition of Wilmington *News Journal*, published on February 17, 1932. "It is an interesting fact that the city of Wilmington likewise is celebrating this year its 100th anniversary. It was chartered as a city in 1832, and has grown with the bank. In both cases progress has been uninterrupted."

Post-War Growth and Innovation

When America joined WWII, WSFS dutifully supported the war effort by purchasing $40,000 of government securities, as it did back during the Civil War. As the **1940s** began with foreboding headlines from Europe, the bank continued its involvement in the community: Advertising home loans and deposit services in the *News Journal* next to its calls for people to buy war bonds. The bank's 110th anniversary in **February of 1942** went ahead without a celebration, due to the weight of the ongoing conflict. When the soldiers finally did return, the bank was there for young families looking to buy their own homes, and residential lending approached $10 million in the immediate post-war period.

By the **late 1950s**, it was time for WSFS to make new footprints by opening its second branch in the fast-growing Fairfax area. The state-of-the-art 40,000 square foot building of stone, aluminum and glass embodied all the latest office trends, including "continuous background music" that played through its cavernous, acoustically-refined halls.

Fairfax Office — Concord Pike, near Murphy Road

From a pamphlet written in **1957** to celebrate WSFS' 125 year anniversary:

"In the intervening years, the Society has constantly sought its customers among those who stand to profit most by regular savings; has protected deposits by unswerving conservative management; has so employed funds entrusted to it so as to return to depositors the highest interest consistent with safety; has never forgotten the fact that the institution exists solely for service to depositors."

Indeed, no matter what was going on in the country at the time— be it the Civil War, financial panics of the late 1800s, World War I, the Great Depression or World War II, WSFS ticked on. Hefty leather-bound minute books, their covers now flaking from years of handling and additional years of storage, tell the story of the month-to-month toils of the Wilmington thrift from the depths of the archives at the Hagley Library. Loans were made to people like Margaret A. Little at 1315 West Third St. for $1,000 in 1915, and Frank B. Hitchcock at 2314 Blvd. for $6,400 in 1919. Harriet E. Blore came in regularly from 1909 to 1926 to have her ledger card stamped, demonstrating that her balance at WSFS increased from $2.88 to $5.52 over time. New board members were approved, and then debated whether to invest the depositors' funds in railroads, U.S. bonds, and more. It was business as usual: The business of serving the hardworking people of that city by the Brandywine.

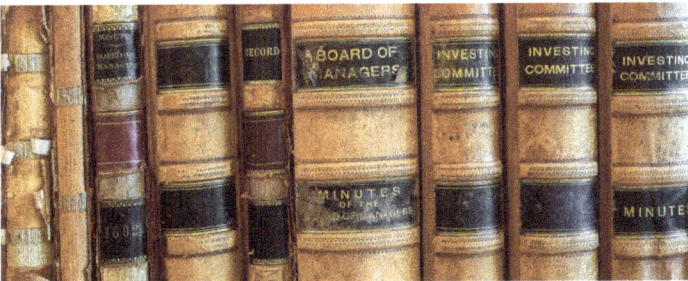

Photo: Floyd Dean—Dean Digital Imaging

A Plan for Posterity

In **1972**, WSFS introduced a little piece of plastic that would shake up banking as everyone knew it. The "Plan Card," as it was called, was believed to be the world's first debit card, enabling funds to be transferred directly from a customer's checking account through a simple point-of-sale transaction. Two percent of the purchase would be deposited directly into the customer's savings account—to WSFS' knowledge, the first cash-back rewards system.

Needless to say, the Plan Card was an enormous hit, compelling industry leaders from as far as New Zealand to come to Delaware to learn more about it. The Plan Package, which combined the first zero-balance checking account with a related savings account, quickly became a favorite among WSFS customers, driving major growth throughout the 1970s and helping the bank break the threshold of 100,000 account relationships.

"In addition to making good business sense, the PLAN has attracted depositors at the growth end of the savings depositor spectrum, those between 25-45 years old and better than average income and education. Over 50% of our PLAN members had no banking relationships with us at all, three years ago," said N. Russell Hartzell Jr., the eighth president of WSFS, in a **1974** progress letter to board members.

Not only was the Plan Card an industry trailblazer, it ignited the spirit of ingenuity within WSFS that would shape the bank forever after. The WSFS of today is a place that thrives on creativity, using it as a means to meet the diverse challenges posed by our rapidly-evolving world.

Banks often seem to operate in the background of day-to-day events, but they are in reality a key component to the modern life cycle. Over almost two centuries, WSFS has helped countless Wilmingtonians to buy their first homes, setting the foundation for young families to grow and thrive. These families, in turn, have sent their children to local schools, and bolstered the city's economy with their contributions. As those young children have grown, WSFS has been there to help them pay for college and for first cars; for small businesses that enrich the local community. And then, as life winds down, WSFS has been there to help the younger generations figure out the next steps. Life needs banks, and banks need life.

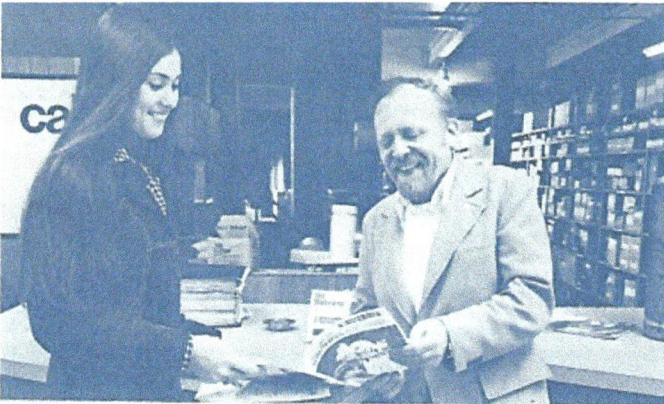

WSFS PLAN Merchant Representative, Sue Everett, chats with Irving Kursh, Bell Supply, Wilmington — one of over 1300 retail outlets that welcomes WSFS PLAN members. Mr. Kursh is leafing through an issue of Savings Fun, distributed bi-monthly to over 16,000 depositor/merchant PLAN members. In addition to offering a 2% Savers Bonus on retail purchases, PLAN merchants also run SAVINGS FUN coupons good for merchandise and service discounts.

Just like the winding path that life can take, WSFS experienced its fair share of growing pains and wayward moments. Some were the result of internal struggles and mistakes; others, the product of external pressures. The decade of the 1970s, where we start our story, was rife with the kinds of issues that would make it hard to remain a first class financial institution.

[3] The Hagley Museum. "The Dupont Company on the Brandywine." Accessed May 17th, 2021. https://www.hagley.org/research/digital-exhibits/dupont-company-brandywine

[4] Scarborough, Paul. [July, 1976]. 200 Years of Delaware Banking, an Exhibition.
[5] https://www.officialdata.org/us/inflation/1832

[6] The building still stands today. WSFS sold it in 2007 as part of the transaction to relocate the headquarters to 500 Delaware Ave. Much of the building was converted to apartments and that famous lobby is now occupied by a branch of a large national bank.

[7] Interestingly, half of the building was rented to another bank organization. In 1955, WSFS took over the whole building.

[8] Scarborough, Paul. [July, 1976]. 200 Years of Delaware Banking, an Exhibition. Wilmington.

[9] When WSFS headquarters was relocated to 500 Delaware Ave in 2007, the mural was removed and donated to the Delaware Historical Society. It remains in storage at this time (2021). The Historical Society plans to eventually restore it and mount it in one of their buildings in the 500 block of North Market Street. We look forward to that day.

Chapter 2
Seeds of Disaster— The Economic Reality for Banks & Thrifts from 1979 to 1990

An overview written by Skip Schoenhals.

What brought about that demand in June 1991, "The Keys Please?" While I'm no economic historian, I did have a front-row seat to the turbulent decades that would spell trouble for WSFS and other banks like it. Since many reading this story may not be familiar with the economic and banking conditions of the 1970s and 80s, the goal of this chapter is to partially set the stage for that infamous June meeting— with a little help from others.

The full economic history of the United States is well beyond the scope of this book and my expertise. To appreciate conditions in the 1970s, 80s and 90s, however, we have to briefly dip our toes in that ocean. We will do that with a quick look at the histories of interest and inflation rates, followed by discussions of how those rates impacted banking institutions and how America responded from a bank regulatory aspect. The perfect storm that led to that ominous June meeting had actually started brewing back in the 1970s. From that perspective, it becomes much easier to understand what happened to WSFS. Those events, coupled with decisions made by management, became a sure recipe for a near bank failure.

In December 1980, the United States' prime interest rate reached an unprecedented height of 21.5%! Digest that for a moment: 21.5%. As the chart below shows, until about 1970, the rate had never been above 5%. In the early part of that decade, it began a relatively steady climb to reach a number that no one had ever dreamed remotely possible. For context, the previous high-water mark had been 12%, for then just a few months in 1974. In the most recent 20 years (2000 to 2021), it again rarely exceeded 5%. So clearly, something dramatic was going on from the middle of the 1970s through the end of the decade, at least in financial markets. For another head-turner, a 30-year mortgage in 1980 would have had a rate of approximately 16%. Care to refinance your home at that rate?

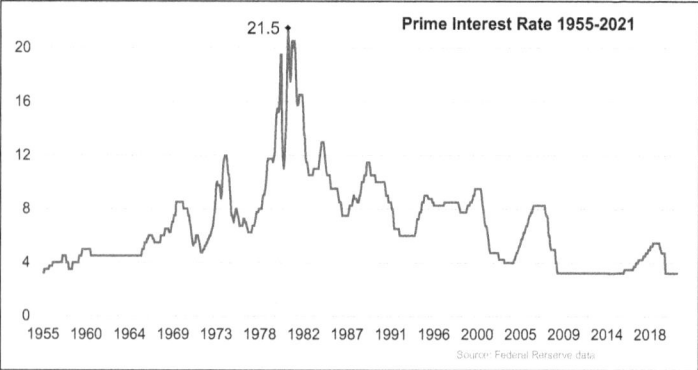

Prime Interest Rate 1955-2021

Source: Federal Reserve data

Chart of Prime Interest Rate

The period of the 1970s and 80s was one of general expansion of the U.S. economy, with one significant interruption from 1973-1975, when the Organization of the Petroleum Exporting Countries (OPEC) chose to quadruple oil prices. At the same time, America was spending heavily on the Vietnam War. These conditions led to 'stagflation' across the country: A strange term that describes the unusual situation of rising unemployment coinciding with rising inflation. Think of gasoline prices jumping by a factor of four— pretty drastic. The issue of inflation was so extreme, in fact, that it led a Republican President (Richard Nixon) to impose price controls on the U.S. economy.

Then, there was a brief recession in 1980— the shortest in American history. Not surprisingly, it was related to interest rates hitting that all-time high of 21.5%. That downturn is often referred to as the "Volcker Shock," a fond way to memorialize the then-Chairman of the Federal Reserve, Paul Volcker. While few would be proud of a recession named after themselves, many consider what Paul Volcker did (in raising interest rates to unheard-of levels) to be one of the most courageous and important acts ever undertaken by the Federal Reserve. While dramatic, the move to high interest rates finally caused ruinous rates of inflation to return to more normal and therefore digestible levels for the economy.

Those rising interest and inflation rates that began in the early 1970s caused, out of necessity, significant revisions in bank regulations. The resulting changes and their unintended consequences caused serious challenges for the entire banking system, but especially for Savings and Loans like WSFS. Proof of the severe impact is in the pudding: Of the 4,039 savings institutions in America in 1980; approximately 1,300 (nearly one third) failed by 1994.[10]

As stated in a 1997 research paper by the Federal Deposit Insurance Corporation (FDIC), developments in the financial markets in the late 1970s and 1980s also tested the commercial banking industry:

"Intrastate banking restrictions were lifted, allowing new players to enter once-sheltered markets, regional banking compacts were established, and direct credit markets expanded. In an environment of high market rates, the development of money market funds and the deregulation of deposit interest rates exerted upward pressures on interest expenses - **particularly for smaller institutions that were heavily dependent on deposit funding."** (Emphasis added)[11]

Some of the developments referenced by the FDIC were the direct result of the rising level of interest rates. Younger readers of this book will likely be surprised to learn that beginning in 1933, banks and thrifts were restricted in the level of interest they could pay on savings deposits, and were prohibited outright from paying any interest on checking account deposits. The restriction was known as Regulation Q, which only applied to deposits held in banks and thrifts. When it was enacted, there were no practical alternative places for the public to place their savings.

However, in the early 1970s, financial markets would find a solution to this dilemma in the creation of money market funds: Mutual funds that only invested in very high-quality liquid investments like U.S. Treasury Notes. While not insured by the FDIC, they were also not subject to Reg Q interest rate limits. So, as interest rates increased in the 70s and 80s, the funds were able to raise the rates they paid for "deposits." While the interest rate limits imposed by Reg Q were also raised, the increases did not keep up with the level to which rates were rising in the general market.

As a result, money began to flow away from the banks and thrifts to money market funds that were paying 'market rates.' This phenomenon was called "disintermediation." In the end, the only effective regulatory response to these issues was to allow interest rate limits under Reg Q to match market rates— a process that began with the passage of the Garn - St. Germain Act in 1982. In addition to moving to market rates on deposits, it expanded allowable banking activities significantly, implementing a variety of changes over the next two to three years. While Reg Q still exists today, the portion of the regulation that limited deposit rates was eliminated for good in 1986.

Why were disintermediation (losing deposits) and rising costs for deposits such a problem for banks and the thrift industry in particular? The answer starts with understanding the primary business of thrifts at that time. Thrifts functioned by attracting deposits (their "raw product") and lending that money in the form of mortgages for home purchases. In those days, mortgages were generally made for a period of about 20 years at a rate that was fixed for the entire life of the mortgage. This model worked fine as long as market rates remained stable. However, as the rates required to attract and keep deposits increased significantly, the 20-year loans continued to earn the same rates they always did.

To illustrate the point, let's look at a hypothetical bank or thrift that primarily provided home mortgages. We will call it Skipton Savings & Loan. In the late 1960s and early 1970s, Skipton was paying between 3% and 5% for all of its deposits. It was making 20-year mortgages at rates of 6% to 7%. Skipton had total assets of $500 million in 1970. For the sake of simplicity, let's assume it did not grow over the next 20 years. Further, as a typical thrift, Skipton would have had about 90% of its assets in home mortgages. So, in 1970 Skipton had an average cost of funds of about 5% and was earning a gross yield on its mortgages of about 7%. The difference of 2% would have been Skipton's gross margin. Out of that it would have paid operating expenses.

As previously stated, all interest rates were moving higher during the 70s, hitting their all-time high in 1980. As a result, Skipton's average cost of deposits would have increased throughout the decade, finally reaching about 8%. At the same time, rates on new mortgages were also increasing, eventually reaching the 16% level mentioned above. That would have produced a nice margin for Skipton, except for one big problem: The mortgages on its books were originally made for 20 years at fixed rates. Therefore, by 1980, Skipton's average yield on assets had only increased to about 8%. Whoops— an average yield on assets of 8% and an average cost of funds of 8% means no gross margin and a big loss after paying operating costs.

This scenario was repeated throughout the nearly 4,000 thrifts that existed in 1980, including WSFS, of course. The situation was so bad that in 1981 all thrifts had combined operating losses of $4.6 billion on total assets of $640 billion, followed in 1982 by a combined loss of $4.1 billion. Obviously, this kind of performance was not sustainable.

Regulators knew they had to do something, and they had two basic choices. The first option was to use regulatory authority to keep bank interest rates below market rates, thereby preserving profits, but creating a huge liquidity problem in the process since those long term fixed-rate loans were not going to leave. Deposits would flow out of banks and thrifts, and the FDIC and Federal Savings and Loan Insurance corporation (FSLIC) would have to close many institutions due to a lack of liquidity— i.e. not having liquid cash to fund withdrawals.

The second path—ultimately the one chosen by Regulators and Congress— was to allow bank deposit rates to move to market, thus plugging the deposit drain. The problem with that was the disappearance of profits for the industry, so there had to be a second step to this solution: Thrifts were given new authority to enter lines of business, lending and investments which had previously been prohibited. Additionally, regulators relaxed capital standards, and even came up with a new class of capital called 'Supervisory Goodwill.' In what is a dramatic oversimplification, this was a class of capital backed only by intangible assets. In the past, intangible assets had been deducted from capital, but with the stroke of a pen, they suddenly counted. The "genius"[12] of this solution was that it allowed stronger thrifts to acquire other thrifts— and to count the goodwill that resulted in any of those acquisitions as capital.

All of these changes were part of the "second step," specifically designed to help the banks and thrifts grow fast enough to overcome the embedded losses in their balance sheets. Once the new lines of business were authorized and the capital requirements relaxed, the regulators eagerly encouraged the banks to start using their new powers to achieve this rapid expansion. In other words, the only way to survive was to grow: and quickly.

Let's go back to Skipton to examine how this plan was designed to work. When we left Skipton it was losing money. Let's assume that loss was 1.5% on assets of $750 million. The theory was that if Skipton could add enough profitable new business by growing rapidly, say over the next two years, it could at least break even. If the net operating margin on those new businesses was 3%, then Skipton would have to add $375 million in new loans and investments to cover those losses embedded in the balance sheet. That would mean a 50% growth in two years, which is unrealistic— but even that would mean the bank was only breaking even. To get to net profit of .5% on assets, a reasonable return would have required even greater growth: a very tough order in two or three years. Nevertheless, that was the idea.[13]

Thrifts were encouraged by the regulatory agencies to enter these new businesses that had higher returns than the more simple (and less risky) home mortgage business. Unfortunately, these more profitable lines had more risk in them. In addition, the primary supervisory agency for thrifts, the Federal Home Loan Bank Board, lacked the knowledge to adequately examine these new types of assets.[14] And guess what? These chickens— these unintended consequences— did come home to roost for the banking sector. The following timeline shows key regulatory changes and the history of corresponding bank failures.

Bank Failures by Year 1979-1993

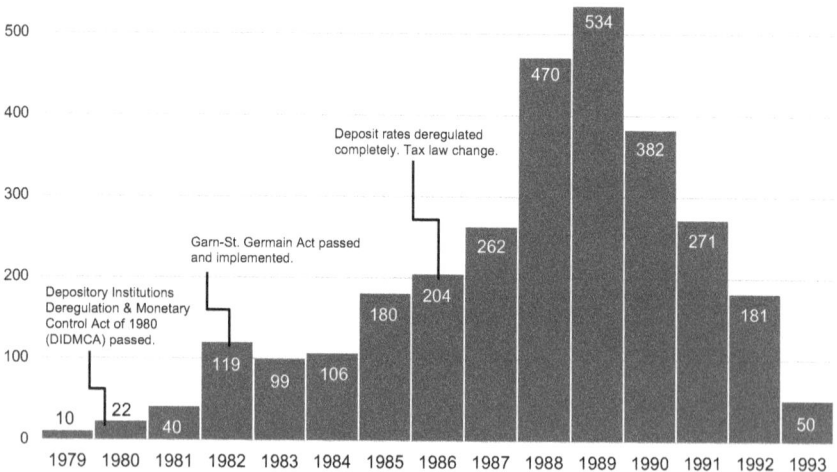

As you can see, many of those chickens landed between 1988 and 1992.

We could go on with this story, but the above data shows the impact of the rising interest rate environment on the health of the thrift industry. While those rates peaked around 1980, spurring an initial increase in failures in the early years of that decade, the supercharged growth that came out of the governmental and regulatory solutions to the crisis ended up creating huge unanticipated ramifications— leading to the real 'Thrift Crisis" of the late 1980s and in which WSFS was caught.

It is estimated that it would have cost the banking insurance agencies about $25 billion to close all the insolvent institutions in the early to mid 1980s, but that was four times the insurance agencies' resources. There was no political will to properly address the problem, so regulators and politicians kicked the can down the road. The cost of that kick: Approximately $160 billion, by the time the problems were resolved in the early 1990s.[15]

 With all that said, let's not be too quick to judge. While we know how things turned out in the end, we don't know what would have happened if an alternative path had been taken.

For me, there is a much deeper point to this story. The original mistake was imposing government-mandated interest rate limits on deposits, which was done for what people thought were reasonable public policy objectives. What those decision makers missed, however, is that the industry was protected from competing with the broad market for deposits. When that protection was removed out of necessity, disaster followed, as the industry was forced to adjust to the real world. Furthermore, during the time that bank/thrift rates were kept below market, savers were denied the opportunity to earn market rates on their savings— an invisible cost.

With an overview of the macroeconomic situation during the 1970s and 80s, we can go back to our narrative: turning our attention to just how WSFS was faring in the midst of the turmoil. While many institutions went out of business, as the above chart demonstrates, those that had strong management or adapted to the rapidly-changing world were able to survive. In the case of WSFS, that survival went beyond its leaders' wildest dreams— but not without first teetering on a deep abyss.

[10] The Federal Deposit Insurance Corporation (FDIC). 1997. History of the Eighties: Lessons for the Future. Vol. 1, An Examination of the Banking Crises of the 1980s and Early 1990s. Washington, DC: FDIC, Page 4.

[11] Ibid

[12] Eventually this form of regulatory capital was eliminated adding to the next 'thrift crisis.'

[13] What actually happened to the industry in general was a combination of accelerated growth and a reduction in interest rates that reduced the embedded losses in the "old" balance sheet.

[14] The Federal Deposit Insurance Corporation (FDIC). 1997. History of the Eighties: Lessons for the Future. Vol. 1, An Examination of the Banking Crises of the 1980s and Early 1990s. Washington, DC: FDIC, Page 169.

[15] Ibid, Page 170.

Chapter 3
Riches to Rags

Despite its firm foundation in the Wilmington community, WSFS was not immune to the effects of the recession in the early 1980s, and more significantly, the impact of dramatically higher interest rates.

At the end of 1979, all was well: The bank had assets totaling $740.5 million and earnings of nearly $6.7 million. But in 1980, the year the prime interest rate hit 21.5%, earnings dropped a shocking 75% to $1.7 million. While that was surely enough bad news to leave board members gasping for air, 1981 would prove even worse— ending in an astounding loss of $5.6 million.

Taken in contrast with the fact that, during the decade of the 70s, income had totaled $25.8 million and no year had ever ended in a loss, it's safe to say that the boardroom suddenly became a very somber place. One can only imagine the discussions that ensued as the negative numbers mounted. The depressing situation would be the catalyst for a leadership change that would affect the bank's future in a dramatically unanticipated way.

On November 8, 1982, J. Walton St. Clair Jr. became the ninth President of WSFS, and the only one in the institution's then-150-year history not to have previously worked within its halls. His telling comments in the 1982 annual report detail the bleak circumstances he encountered at the very beginning of his tenure:

"1982 was a difficult year for the thrift industry, and the Savings Fund was no exception. However, interest rates began to fall in the last half of the year and December brought the new money market instrument. The new instrument, a product of deregulation, is a mixed blessing. We can now compete with the money funds, but our overall cost of funds is higher.

"The first eleven months of the year ended with a decline in deposits of $26 million. In December, deposits increased by $58 million, thanks to the Insured Money Market Investment Account which brought in $44 million of those new savings."

Regardless of the turnaround in deposit flows late in the year, 1982 ended even worse than 1981 with a total loss of $7.2 million. Undoubtedly, these startling numbers were a primary cause of concern for the new management. In appointing St. Clair to the bank's top position, the board hoped that he would be able to tackle the serious challenges that high interest rates had imposed on the thrift industry. But as the government lifted national restrictions on banks and encouraged them to diversify their sources of income, WSFS took a dive into uncharted waters. It all began with the hiring of three new senior executives: one each for lending, marketing and administrative services.

"Walt pulled in people, all commercial bankers from all different areas of expertise, pulled together a management team," recalls T.K. Kerstetter, WSFS president and COO from 1982-1990. "The goal was to make this mutual savings bank operate like a commercial bank, and then have the opportunity to take it public."

Jerry Holbrook, controller of WSFS at the time, remembers that life at the bank revolved around the following mantra: "We've got to grow the company. We've got to get earnings up."

"We had a fair number of consultants, investment bankers and the like, presenting to management and the board about different kinds of strategies," he said. "Those guys had a lot of ideas, a lot of new kinds of things they wanted to change culturally."

The WSFS leadership team had faith that new growth and diversification would reverse the barrage of losses the bank had endured (remember the 'famous' Skipton Savings & Loan from the previous chapter). As they worked to bring their vision to fruition, much about the old WSFS would change. A new chapter was beginning.

Making Moves

As the next few years marched on, the bank became involved in new sectors: Automobile and equipment leasing, mortgage banking, and, most significantly, commercial and residential real estate lending and direct development. The new management saw key opportunities to increase income in each of these spheres, but their real aspiration was to become a 'vertical' player in the residential real estate market: A status they felt would produce significant opportunities to increase income. In 1985, WSFS formed Star States Development Company—a real estate development subsidiary— to achieve that aim, and also acquired a successful residential real estate brokerage firm, The B. Gary Scott Company. If all went well, this would allow the bank to develop the land, sell the homes and then finance them.

One more important move was the conversion of the bank to a Federal Savings & Loan Charter. Along with allowing more flexibility and higher lending limits, this shift would eventually allow the bank to go public— a key future goal of the new leaders. They also formed a holding company under the name Stars States Financial Corp: Setting the stage for the plan to grow WSFS' footprint well beyond its traditional territory of Wilmington and Delaware. After all, a bank with "Wilmington" in its name was not likely to have much curb appeal in Pennsylvania, Maryland or New Jersey, so they dropped it in favor of a more geographically-neutral title. While there is no official record, it seems logical to guess that they thought the name of the bank itself would eventually become Star States as well.

As the following table demonstrates, these initiatives— along with an improving interest rate environment—revived the company's performance for a time. After the $7.2 million loss in 1982, earnings began to recover:

KEY OPERATING RESULTS 1983 THROUGH 1987

Year	Net Income/(Loss)*
1983	$(3,494,000)
1984	$(580,000)
1985	$ 2,881,000
1986	$ 3,050,000
1987	$ 8,012,000

*Includes extraordinary items from Tax Loss Carry forwards of $700,000, $1.6 million, and $3.3 million in 1985 through 1987, respectively.

As management had hoped, this crucial recuperation finally allowed them to achieve their principal goal of converting the bank to a public company, which they did in November of 1986. The early signs were promising: The offering raised a hearty $42.5 million, which nearly doubled the bank's net worth and provided lots of fuel (capital) to support growth.

"The net proceeds…will be used for general corporate purposes including supporting lending, investment and other activities and possible expansion of such activities, including through mergers and acquisitions," stated page 13 of the Offering Circular, dated November 26, 1986. And so it was.

For the next few months, the halls of WSFS buzzed with excitement. In December of 1986, an article on the front page of the bank's publication for Associates captured those sentiments: "Before a standing-room-only crowd at the Wilmington Hilton, WSFS President and Chief Executive Officer J. Walton St. Clair Jr. described the plans for the future of WSFS."

The years 1987 and 1988 would see a slew of important acquisitions and developments. In August 1988, WSFS announced the agreement to purchase Diversified Investment Group (DING), better known as Fidelity Federal Savings and Loan Association, located in northeast Philadelphia. A few months later, in November, it acquired Anderson Leasing in Elkton, Maryland. And, just before 1988 rolled to a close— in what would turn out to be a most audacious move—the bank announced plans for a glossy new headquarters building in Wilmington's Rodney Square: a prime location for what the *News Journal* dubbed a "monument to WSFS."

And what a monument it would be. At a proposed 30 stories, the tower promised to be the tallest in the state— a far cry from the bank's first headquarters below Wilmington's old town hall.

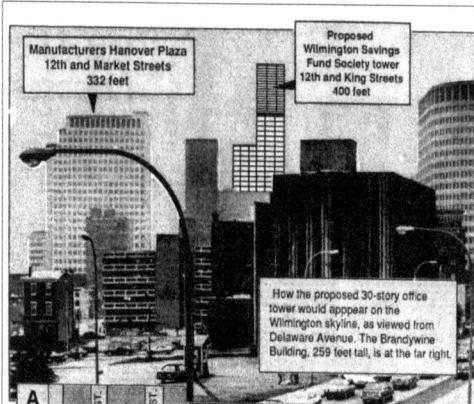

Manufacturers Hanover Plaza
12th and Market Streets
332 feet

Proposed
Wilmington Savings
Fund Society tower
12th and King Streets
400 feet

How the proposed 30-story office tower would apppear on the Wilmington skyline, as viewed from Delaware Avenue. The Brandywine Building, 259 feet tall, is at the far right.

A Manufacturer's Hanover building; 332 feet tall

B Fire station city will sell to Wilmington Parking Authority

C Proposed 400-foot-tall, 30-story office building.

J. Walton St. Clair Jr., president and CEO of Wilmington Savings Fund Society, stands next to an artist's rendering of the 30-story building which will become its headquarters.

30-story office tower proposed

Wilmington building would be state's tallest

By JOHN O'NEILL
Staff reporter

Wilmington's skyline is on the rise again.

Delle Donne & Associates Inc. and Wilmington Savings Fund Society said Wednesday they'll build a 30-story office tower — the tallest to date in the state — on the downtown block bounded by King, French 11th and 12th streets.

Delle Donne said his firm had considered putting up a 300,000-square-foot building on the property before WSFS decided to join the project. Now 450,000 square feet is planned.

"We just made the building bigger," Delle Donne said.

WSFS will own the building with Delle Donne, and set up new headquarters on 250,000 square feet of the building, roughly the bottom 10 floors, and possibly take the top floor, too.

Delle Donne also will move its offices to the building from its current site at 800 Delaware Ave. The development firm will take 60,000 square feet of space.

Construction of the 400-foot-tall building will start next spring and finish in early 1991. It will cost $70 million to build and dwarf the nearby Brandywine Building, at 259 feet, and the recently completed Manufacturers Hanover Plaza, 332 feet high.

The base of the proposed building will include a 200-car garage.

Homeless shelter will need to be relocated. **A6**

to be run by the Wilmington Parking Authority.

The authority also announced plans for an 800-car parking garage on the northern end of the same block.

According to Wilmington Mayor Daniel Frawley, "Without structured parking, the [building] transaction would not have taken place."

Frawley said Wilmington will sell the former city fire station at 12th and French to the authority for the proposed 800-car garage. The fire station, now used as a shelter for the homeless, has been assessed at $2 million.

The details of the fire station sale have not been completed, according to authority Chairman Frank Wharton. He said the authority probably will buy the ground rights to the fire station, and the city probably will keep the air, or development rights, to the property.

Wharton said the authority is negotiating for property between the fire station and the proposed building, but will build a garage on the site of the old station even if the additional land is not available.

See BUILDING — A6

Building

• Continued from A1

able.

Linking the tower's garage with one on the station site would be more desirable. But, Wharton said, the station site alone should be adequate for an 800-car garage, although the garage might have to be cantilevered over adjacent streets.

The 250,000 square feet of space that WSFS will occupy is about 75,000 square feet more than its current administrative space.

"It's a great opportunity for us to consolidate operations," said J. Walton St. Clair Jr., president of

WSFS. "Our organization is presently housed in various facilities throughout the city and county."

The WSFS administrative offices at Ninth and Market streets will move to the new building, leaving that bank building and offices to function as a branch. St. Clair said. Moving to the new building will be administrative offices on Old Philadelphia Pike in Claymont, in the Marine Midland Building adjacent to the bank on the Market Street Mall, and in the First Federal Savings Building along Walnut Street.

New York architect Edward Larrabee Barnes will design the building, according to Ernest F Delle Donne, president of Delle

Donne & Associates.

"He's probably one of the top five architects in the world," Delle Donne said.

Larrabee designed the IBM headquarters in Manhattan, among other buildings, Delle Donne said.

"In all honesty, I do prefer building a headquarters building," said Delle Donne, whose firm built the Chase Manhattan building at 802 Delaware Ave.

"The bottom floors of a building are the hardest to lease," Delle Donne said, noting WSFS' commitment to take the lower floors of the new tower.

"As of now, it looks as if they will finance the entire venture as

well," he added.

WSFS finances about 90 percent of Delle Donne & Associates' projects, he said. WSFS loaned Delle Donne roughly 70 percent of the $4.3 million his firm used to buy the six tenths of an acre on which the new building will sit. Delle Donne bought the property from Provident Mutual Life Insurance Co. of Philadelphia.

Frawley cited the property tax and employment benefits to come with the new building, and underscored the parking authority and city roles in setting up the project.

"This particular transaction took well over two years to organize and execute," Frawley said.

See explanation regarding reproduced newspaper stories on Page 7.

A Problematic Path

While all of these developments portrayed a company with a sunny future, there were dark storm clouds rapidly forming on the horizon. The early warning signs of this tempest can best be visualized by tracking WSFS' 'provision for loan losses'— the money the bank set aside each year to cover anticipated bad loans.

In 1984 and '85, before going public, the provision was $600,000 each year. In 1986, it doubled to $1.2 million. Although that sounds like a substantial increase, it wasn't terribly alarming for a rapidly-growing company looking to prepare for any eventuality. When coupled with a 50% jump in 1987 to $1.8 million, though, it became evident that trouble was brewing. Indeed, it was not just a red flag: It became a bomb in 1988, when the provision leapt almost fourfold to more than $6.5 million. By 1989, it was through the roof— a whopping $14.0 million, which represented nearly 1.4% of loans. Something was clearly very, very wrong.

The sirens really started to wail when WSFS received a transmittal letter from its primary regulator at the time— the Federal Home Loan Bank Board's Office of the Supervisory Agent, dated May 9, 1988. It conveyed the following from the exam conducted on March 22, 1988:

"We express serious concern regarding the increase in both the dollar amount and severity of classified assets since the February 2, 1987 examination report."

That was just the beginning. Things got worse.

On November 3, 1988, the regulator sent another transmittal letter based on the exam on July 5 of that year. Again, seasoned bankers will recognize major warning lights here— a follow-up exam in less than four months indicates that the regulator is extremely concerned. In this case, the regulator's "concern" was more like true distress: The letter contained five numbered points, four of which were pointedly unfavorable. They started with phrases like, "The board's failure to implement...;" "We are concerned...;" "We wish to advise the board...;" and "...please advise us of the corrective actions taken..."

The full letter appears on next page, but these brief summaries leave no doubt about the regulators' thoughts.

So, what happened? This trajectory of loan loss provisions tells the all-too-common story of banks that attempt to grow rapidly through the aggressive expansion of lending in areas where they have little prior experience. Many of the borrowers who came to WSFS when it moved into commercial real estate loans had originally been denied by other banks— and, as results would eventually prove, for good reason. Combined with the beginning of a national slump in the real estate market, this meant that the new investments and acquisitions proved much less profitable— and far more problematic— than the company had anticipated.

An analysis of WSFS' earnings over those same years tracks quite well with the early warning signs from the loan loss provisions. The excitement of going public in '86 was short-lived: Profits declined from $8 million in 1987 to $6 million in 1988, and then disappeared altogether in 1989 with an outright loss of $5.8 million.

The real crunch wouldn't come until 1990, but we get ahead of our story. There was another pressing matter on the table— well, actually on the ground.

James D. Roy
Principal Agent

Richard B. Pow
Chief Agent

Patrick J. Coyne
Agent

William C. Eayre
Agent

Federal Home Loan Bank Board
Office of Supervisory Agent
Third District

November 3, 1988

Terrence J. Cronin
Agent

Nancy J. Lyle
Agent

John F. Roche
Agent

Roy M. Legleitner
Agent-Applications

Board of Directors
Wilmington Savings Fund Society, FSB
838 Market Street
Wilmington, DE 19899

FHLBB No. 7938

Dear Board Members:

RE: Report of Examination Dated July 5, 1988

We enclose a copy of the above-captioned Report of Examination("Report") which is to be reviewed in its entirety within thirty (30) days at a regular or special meeting of the board. Further, within forty-five (45) days of receipt of this letter, you are requested to submit certified excerpts from the official board minutes, in triplicate, setting forth your response to the Report and the various concerns discussed below:

1. We are pleased to acknowledge the favorable GAP and capital positions maintained by the institution as noted in the Report.

2. The board's failure to implement a management succession plan is a cause of concern for us. The absence of a management succession plan is particularly significant in light of the recent level of turnover that has occurred within the institution's executive management. Accordingly, we request that the board submit to this Office a specific plan regarding management succession.

   In addition, we are concerned over the criticism contained at page 5 of the Report, relating to the board's failure to ensure that the institution maintain current information regarding the institution's involvement with outside projects or ventures. We request that the board implement appropriate reporting procedures to ensure that current information regarding ongoing projects or ventures is maintained at the institution. Please submit a copy of the proposed reporting procedures with your response.

3. We are concerned about the increasing level of the institution's classified assets, as described by the examiner on Report pages 9, 10, 11 and A-12.1 thru A-13.2. In your response, please advise us of the board's strategy and specific actions to be taken to effect a reduction in the level of classified assets, particularly, the institution's plans for resolving the recently classified ""Hannon/Goldberg", and Mybev" credits that are discussed on pages 10 and A-12.9 thru A-12.13 of the Report. Further, we request a status report as to each of the classified loans, which should include, at a minimum, a discussion of the specific collection efforts made regarding each loan.

4. We wish to advise the Board that Insurance Regulation § 561.16c (d) (1) requires an institution to establish or increase general allowances for loan losses when an examiner classifies one or more assets, or portions thereof, substandard or doubtful, and the examiner has determined that existing valuation allowances are inadequate. The examiner states, on page 21 of the Report, that the institution's general loan loss reserves "is approximately $6.7 million short of being adequate." We note that the same conclusion is contained on page 4-4 of the May 31, 1988 FDIC Report of Examination. We, therefore, request that the board confirm that the general reserve shortfall has been corrected and advise us of its plan to maintain adequate general loan loss reserves in the future. In the event the board believes a different amount to be appropriate, we request to be apprised of that amount and, to be provided with a detailed analysis supporting same.

5. We have reviewed the examiner's comments on page 13 of the Report concerning deficiencies in the institution's Investment Policy, and concur with the examiner's recommendations for improvement of said policy. In your response, please advise us of the corrective actions taken to eliminate the reported deficiencies.

   Please acknowledge receipt of this letter and Report by completing and returning the enclosed postcard.

Sincerely yours,

Patrick J. Coyne

PJC: as
Enclosures

55

The Hole in the Ground

Amidst all the inner turmoil plaguing WSFS in 1989— and despite the regulators' concerns— the bank stuck with the plan to break ground that year for its much-discussed new headquarters building. The formal ceremony took place in November with plenty of fanfare, but the euphoria would not last. Initial construction activity was followed by the stark realization that the bank had quite literally dug itself into a hole. Less than six months later, with only the initial footings in place, the board stopped construction amid significant signals from the regulator.

For one thing, the $70 million price tag certainly got the skeptics talking. "How can a bank that's just reported a $9 million loss afford it?" Read an unattributed quote in the *News Journal*. "It's a high risk," said a competitor. "It could bury them."

As 1990 rolled forward, the site would continue to invite a flood of criticism and speculation from Wilmingtonians and out-of-towners alike, who stared down at a gaping trench and wondered what would become of the storied old thrift. It became infamously known as the "Hole in the Ground"— in some ways, a metaphor for what the bank was also missing on its balance sheet, and a painful reminder to management that they'd need a pretty big shovel to dig themselves out.

Business

WSFS building tower of controversy

At prime site on square, no corners cut

By JOHN O'NEILL
Staff reporter

WILMINGTON — The developers of the Star States Tower paid their architect $1.4 million.

New York architect Edward Larrabee Barnes — who designed IBM's headquarters in Manhattan — cost $400,000 more than the average architect, said Ernest Delle Donne, president of Delle Donne & Associates Inc., developer of the 21-story, $70 million office tower.

"Barnes works personally on only two projects a year," Delle Donne said. "He doesn't even negotiate his price."

Barnes was chosen by both Delle Donne and Star States Corp., partners in the tower, to design a building appropriate for the headquarters of Wilmington Savings Fund Society, Star States' principal subsidiary. The partners also judged Barnes' skills appropriate for a site everyone agrees is among the most valuable left in Wilmington.

"Rodney Square is center stage. I wanted to hide behind an architect on this project," Delle Donne said. "Barnes gives this building a pedigree that takes the onus off of me."

Choosing a major architect was not the partners' only splurge. The tower will have a lobby 40 feet tall, taller than any lobby in Wilmington and 15 feet taller than the lobby of the new One Christina Centre building at Fourth and Walnut streets. "We spent an extra million dollars on the lobby," Delle Donne said.

The building must be costly to succeed, Delle Donne said. Businesses locate around Rodney Square for prestige, he said. They want distinctive office space and they expect the high rents needed to pay for the quality. The high quality of the tower will help to draw tenants, Delle Donne said, and ensure the property's value.

"If you want to be next to Rodney Square and the courthouse, you're willing to pay more," agreed Pete Davisson, a real estate agent with Jackson-Cross Co.

The value of property diminishes as one moves away from the square, Davisson said, adding "there is a direct correlation between what you get for ground and what you get in rental rates." Delle Donne paid $4.3 million for the land, borrowing $2.5 million from WSFS toward the price.

Nearness to Rodney Square does enhance a property's value, real estate appraiser David Wilk agreed, because the square is within Wilmington's busiest financial district. The highest land values in the district are near the square along the 10th, 11th and 12th street corridor, which give access to Interstate 95, Wilk said.

Parking also enhances the value of land around the square, he said.

Star States Tower has parking because the Wilmington Parking Authority is building an 800-car garage on the northern end of the same block. The authority has wanted to build a garage in the area of the WSFS tower for a long time, said Frank Wharton, until recently the authority's board chairman.

The authority chose to build the garage now in part because Wilmington officials offered to sell it the city's fire station at King and 12th streets. The land under this station — which the authority will buy for about $2 million — helped to make the garage feasible, Wharton said.

The city offered the land to the authority because it knew parking was needed to keep WSFS in the city, said J. Brian Murphy, city commerce director.

Keeping WSFS in the city retains a major employer and the city taxes charged the bank's workers. "Also, it's good to keep the [development] momentum going," Murphy said. The city has kept the right to develop on top of the garage at 12th and King streets.

Delle Donne said he expects to save $4 million in city and New Castle County tax breaks.

The city promised Star States and Delle Donne a five-year abatement on all property taxes. The county gave a 10-year property-tax abatement, which declines 10 percent a year through the 11th year.

"That gives us a $1.50- to $2-a-square-foot advantage over an old building [which must pay real estate taxes]," Delle Donne said.

WSFS will lend the Star States and Delle Donne partnership the $70 million it will cost to build the tower. According to Securities and Exchange Commission documents, WSFS will borrow the money from the Federal Home Loan Bank Board of Pittsburgh and may sell parts of the loan to other banks. Star States will own 78 percent of the new building; Delle Donne & Associates, 22

See TOWER E3

FROM PAGE E1

percent. WSFS is taking 225,000 square feet of space on 12 floors, roughly 55 percent of the building, according to WSFS Chairman J. Walton St. Clair Jr. The bank will own half of the remaining space and expects to defray its own rent with rental income from this other space.

On average, a new building breaks even on its cost if it leases 75 percent of its space, Davisson said. Because WSFS is taking 225,000 square feet of space, the tower will have to lease another 125,000 square feet to break even.

Davisson said he thinks this is feasible given the average yearly rate at which space has been taken up in the central business district. One variable that is not known is whether other new buildings will come on line to compete with the Star States Tower, Davisson said.

Delle Donne is convinced the tower will lease, whatever the competition, because of its quality.

"This will be the finest structure on Rodney Square, period. You can't make any more Rodney Square," he said. The building is better than other Rodney Square buildings because of amenities such as parking. Its nearness to the courthouse makes it an attractive spot for law firms moreover.

"The law firm that doesn't live in our building when we open in 1991 will 10 years later," Delle Donne said.

Delle Donne also argued the attractiveness of the site — in particular the high certainty that it will lease due to its prime location — reduces the building's cap rate, a calculation of the return on investment any future buyer of the building must be promised and a banking indicator of the value of a building.

Delle Donne said the tower's cap rate will be lower than the rate of a building more distant from Rodney Square, an indication that it is less risky, and this lower rate allows the partnership to finance the project with less costly money.

Choosing a major architect was not the only splurge. The tower will have a lobby 40 feet tall. "We spent an extra million dollars on the lobby," said developer Ernest Delle Donne.

An artist's rendering of the Star States Tower on Wilmington's Rodney Square.

WSFS: Some critics say bank's building a risky business

By MARCIA MING
Staff reporter

WILMINGTON — While the people at Wilmington Savings Fund Society were launching balloons Thursday to celebrate the groundbreaking on their new headquarters building on Rodney Square, critics shook their heads in disbelief.

Named for the holding company that owns WSFS, the proposed Star States Tower will occupy the last prime location available on Rodney Square. Critics seem to have no quarrel with the location – which alone should favor the building's success — but they raise serious questions about whether WSFS should be involved in the venture.

"How can a bank that just reported a $9 million loss for the third quarter move ahead with such a project?" one banker asked. "How can they afford it, in view of what's been in the paper?"

Bankers and others, knowledgeable about real estate, question whether the new building is a good business decision for WSFS and its parent, Star States Corp., given the bank's growing problem with bad loans, the current weakness in the real estate market and forecasts of a possible recession in 1990.

However, Star States officials say the building does not involve a lot of risk, and is the best way to meet the company's space needs into the 21st century.

The issue is so sensitive that virtually no one would comment for attribution, but their concerns were supported by documents filed by the bank with the Securities and Exchange Commission.

"It's a high risk," said a competitor. "It could bury them."

One observer called Star States Tower an "ego" building, proposed by the bank's management in response to towering structures competitors have erected in recent years.

By regulatory standards, WSFS is a healthy institution. With shareholders' equity of more than $88.6 million, the savings bank has an equity-to-assets ratio of 6.12 percent. That is well above the 3 percent required by its charter and 6 percent needed to qualify for insurance by bank standards with the Federal Deposit Insurance Corp.

What's causing so much concern is the sharp rise in the bank's non-performing loans since 1985.

Non-performing loans are ones the borrower can no longer fulfill the original contractual terms of — typically, payments of interest or principal overdue by 90 days or more.

In its 1987 annual report, WSFS reported $2.16 million in non-performing loans for the period ending Dec. 31, 1985. The same report showed the numbers rising to $6.85 million by the end of 1986, and $17.5 million by the end of 1987.

Subsequent reports show the level of problem loans reaching $18.6 million by the end of 1988, before rising to $54.0 million by the third quarter of 1989.

In December 1988, Star States took a hit against earnings to boost its reserve for bad loans by $4.8 million.

The bank said the special provision was largely the result of foreclosures involving two of the bank's major non-performing loans.

WSFS wrote off $2.8 million in loans, after foreclosing against the Alyson's Restaurant at 1800 Naamans Road and St. Michael's Marina and Hotel in St. Michael's, Md. It added the other $2 million to its loan loss reserve to bring the fund back up to a healthy level, relative to

See WSFS — E2

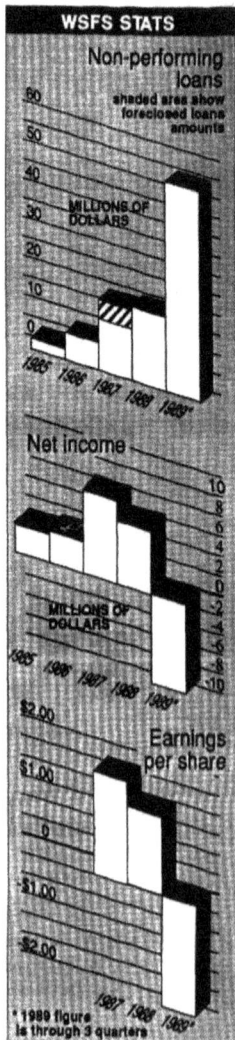

WSFS STATS

Non-performing loans
shaded area show foreclosed loans amounts

MILLIONS OF DOLLARS

60
50
40
30
20
10
0

1985 1986 1987 1988 1989*

Net income
10
8
6
4
2
0
-2
-4
-6
-8
-10

MILLIONS OF DOLLARS

1985 1986 1987 1988 1989*

Earnings per share
$2.00
$1.00
0
-$1.00
-$2.00

1987 1988 1989*

* 1989 figure is through 3 quarters

The News Journal/ HOWARD JOHNSON

other outstanding loans.

The loan charge-offs came in a strong quarter, resulting in a 22 percent decline in earnings, although the bank still managed to earn $2.1 million for the quarter and $6 million for the year.

Star States didn't fare as well in the most recent quarter, when more problem loans forced the bank to take another large hit against earnings to boost its reserve by $10.3 million. The result was a net loss for the third quarter of $9.0 million or $1.92 a share.

J. Walton St. Clair Jr., Star States' chairman and chief executive officer, says the bank cannot discuss its relationship with customers and declined to comment on projects that sources link to the bank's bad-loan problems.

In SEC filings, Star States said it is trying to sell both the restaurant, which is no longer operating, and the marina, which is. The bank said it also had foreclosed on other past-due consumer loans and mobile homes.

Also, Star States said one of its joint ventures — representing a $12.5 million investment for the company, and thought to be Brandywine Park Condominiums — is selling its residential units at a rate slower than projected.

Observers also note that WSFS has outstanding loans on the renovated Pennsylvania Building behind the Amtrak station and on the old YWCA building, two projects that remain largely empty.

Any bank can get into trouble because of bad loans, as most Delaware bankers readily admit. But cautious, conservative bank officials avoid taking on unusual risks in times of trouble. As a rule, they tighten lending standards and cut costs as they try to stabilize and contain the damage.

Most bank officials interviewed by The News Journal said they would not consider a headquarters building or a merger at a time when the economy is uncertain and their problem loans were growing.

Star States recently announced that it still plans to acquire Diversified Investment Group Inc., which owns Fidelity Federal Savings and Loan Association of Philadelphia, in a deal valued at about $24 million. Originally, the Delaware company agreed to pay $28.8 million for the smaller thrift, but the deal fell through last summer when the thrifts' earnings dropped and Star States tried to renegotiate the deal.

Extra space needed

St. Clair and Star States President Thomas K. Kerstetter said they don't view the building as a big risk. They say they will need extra space from 1991 when all of the leases except one will expire. They also said they will need space for expansion through the year 2000.

One real estate expert suggested that WSFS may have committed for a lot more space than it needs. Wilmington Trust Co., with more than $3 billion in assets and income from a giant trust operation, has between 900 and 1,000 people working in similar space. Bank of Delaware occupies about 230,000 square feet in two downtown buildings with 750 to 800 employees.

With $1.4 billion in assets, WSFS plans to consolidate about 380 workers from five sites in about 225,000 square feet of space. About 200 of the employees will be moving from two buildings that Star States owns free and clear with no mortgage. What that suggests is that the bank may be moving from a situation of having a fairly low overhead to significantly higher costs. And as one source pointed out, many of the thrifts the federal government is closing right now were building new headquarters buildings.

Growing at an average rate of about 11 percent a year for the last five years, it could take a decade or more for the bank to reach a size where the income from its business would adequately support the space.

Even if money is no object, most banking companies are striving to become low-cost producers because of the increased competition. WSFS would be bucking that trend by taking on more space than it needs. Of course the bank could decide to lease some of the space but that would be competing with the 50 percent of the project the developer plans to lease and other unleased office space in the area.

St. Clair, Star States' chairman, says the bank has outgrown its present space and would need to move even if it hadn't planned the new site. He said the cost of the bank's space on Rodney Square will not be much greater than what the bank would have to pay if, for example, it moved to new, leased quarters in the suburbs.

That's because the bank will be paying less than the market rate for its space in the new tower while, as a partner in the building, it will earn income from space leased to other tenants.

In addition to the discount, the bank also will receive tax abatements from the city and a parking structure provided by the Wilmington Parking Authority.

The lure of a building

There also is the intangible benefit that will come from having an attractive, signature building, says Star States board member Thomas Shea. According to Kerstetter, an attractive headquarters will help in the recruitment of employees and development of new customers.

No one disputes the argument that the tower will be a premier building on one of the best sites available. Because it's a prime site, Ernest Delle Donne of Delle Donne & Associates Inc., the developer, says he will be able to blow away the competition on Rodney Square.

The building will be easier to lease than buildings off the square, Delle Donne said, making it less of a risk for owners. It's the difference between buying a building in Manhattan and buying one in a less prestigious area, such as the Queens, he said.

The risk with the bank is whether it really needs as much space as it's committed for in the short run and whether it needs to pay as much for the space it needs as the Star States Tower will cost.

Some investors who bought Star States' stock banking on its attractiveness as a takeover target are not happy about the building and have expressed their concerns to the bank, Kerstetter said. The added debt would make the stock less attractive than it otherwise would have been when national interstate banking takes effect in 1990, stockholders say.

Most of the big Delaware banks already have been acquired. WSFS was one of the most attractive targets remaining because of its large statewide customer base and relatively low price tag.

The only other big bank available would be Wilmington Trust, which has vowed to remain independent and which would be fairly expensive to acquire because of its long streak of record profits.

The fact that some Star States stockholders oppose the building is significant because the largest stockholders, big institutional investors, hold more shares than the bank's management and directors. WSFS went public in 1986. Capital raised from selling stock helped WSFS achieve a healthy level of regulatory capital.

Star States' largest stockholders include: WMG Co.; Templeton Galbraith & Hansberger, the parent company of the Templeton worldwide fund group; Wells Fargo Bank; Wilmington Trust; Meridian Bancorp and Mellon Bank Corp.

The Hole in the Ground. Leo S. Matkins for the *News Journal*.

It would stay that way for nearly five years, until the bank sold the land to MBNA—one of the very successful credit card banks that made a home for itself in Wilmington in the early 1980s. (In 2006, MBNA was acquired by Bank of America, which continues to have a significant presence in downtown Wilmington).

Nick Ketcha, former New York regional director of the FDIC, had this to say about the unfinished construction site: "I remember thinking something along the lines of, 'Well, they've dug the hole and they've got one foot firmly planted in it.'"

A Troublesome End to the '80s

In January of 1990— 18 months before the disastrous June 19 meeting where our story began— Walt St. Clair looked back on the previous year and told the *News Journal* that 1989 had been "a challenging year in positioning the company to move ahead."

That assessment was definitely an understatement: Non-performing loans had increased by a whopping 180% that year, compelling the bank to enter into a formal agreement with its regulator called a Memorandum of Understanding. While not the most serious enforcement act that could have been taken, it spelled specific steps that the bank was required to take to improve prospects for the future.

"When we got into the late '80s, things were pretty bad and we were getting a lot of bad press," remembers Chip Clifton, then working in Branch Operations.

"At one point, we thought that there might be a run on the bank. I can remember sitting in Walt St. Clair's office talking to Brooks Armored Car. We'd made arrangements to have $30 million in cash on hand sitting in a Brooks truck at an undisclosed location, and my job was to look at branch totals like every five or 10 minutes. If I saw anything drop, I'd have to direct the car to whatever office appeared to be running out of money. So that was pretty scary."

With all of these troubles, WSFS leadership had no choice but to rein in the intense acquisition and diversification efforts that had been their central strategy for growth. But the bank's deep-seeded problems would not be a quick fix. Bad loans continued to plague the institution, sucking away money at a terrifying rate.

Growth and diversification came at a costly price to Star States

By PETER OSBORNE
Staff reporter

WILMINGTON — As they so often do, the numbers tell the story for Star States Corp. almost as articulately as the company's outgoing president summed up his tenure.

"You could probabiy make the case now that the company made some poor judgments in expanding its vision too quickly," said Thomas K. Kerstetter, who joined Chairman and Chief Executive Officer J. Walton St. Clair in resigning late Friday afternoon after the parent of Wilmington Savings Fund Society announced a $26.6 million loss. "In retrospect, we probably grew and diversified faster than we should have."

The balance sheet was simple back in 1982 when St. Clair arrived on the scene. There was no Star States holding company and WSFS had only two subsidiaries — First Leaseplan Corp. and WSFS Mortgage Co.

Today, Star States Corp. has eight subsidiaries, including WSFS, B. Gary Scott Realtors and a Philadelphia area thrift.

Assets didn't cross the $1 billion threshold until 1985; today they're $1.6 billion. During the mid-'80s, the provision for loan losses was consistently $600,000; today it stands at more than $14 million.

And Star States wrote off bad loans totaling $7.4 million in the second quarter alone. By comparison; the company didn't write off that many loans in total in the six years between 1982 and 1987. Since then, the floodgates have opened; Star States wrote off $5.7 million in bad loans in 1988 and $9.2 million in 1989.

ANALYSIS

Bank officials, investors and analysts agree those numbers make it difficult to implement any meaningful expense-reduction program. At the end of 1989, operating expenses had soared to 2.49 percent of average assets; experts say strong thrifts operate with expenses at about 1.5 percent of assets. Sixty jobs, or 10 percent of WSFS's workforce, have been cut in the past 10 months.

Others say privately the efforts to slice expenses were exacerbated by the fact that the cuts had to come from busi-

> "You could probably make the case that the company made some poor judgments."
>
> THOMAS K. KERSTETTER

nesses St. Clair and Kerstetter introduced in the first place and to which they no doubt had some emotional ties.

Still, the problems seem confined to businesses outside of WSFS. Star States in recent years sought new sources of fee income, acquiring subsidiaries in such businesses as real estate and insurance brokerage, real estate development and motor vehicle and equipment leasing.

The plan centered on a vertically integrated approach to real estate development. In April, St. Clair conceded that

what worked in theory didn't always work in practice.

Both Kerstetter, who will stay on to run day-to-day operations until a new chief executive is hired, and interim Chairman Charles G. Cheleden emphasized that depositors were safe, a claim generally supported by the numbers.

As of June 30, WSFS was in compliance with the federal Office of Thrift Supervision's tangible capital requirements, but did not meet its risk-based or core-capital requirements.

The problem loans affect the entire balance sheet. In 1989 alone the $36.2 million in non-performing loans represented a potential $2.7 million in additional net interest income. They also depress capital levels. Star States was meeting all its capital requirements when it signed an OTS agreement in June that offers targets and deadlines for reducing loans and adding capital. Star States still is in compliance with the agreement.

Kerstetter and St. Clair say they started talking about resigning on Thursday, but they likely were living on borrowed time. No matter how strong the core WSFS banking franchise is, the board of directors needed to do something to rebuild investor confidence.

The rumors all week of a terrible second quarter and impending resignations seemed more credible when Star States told reporters it would hold a press conference at 3:30 p.m. on Friday. That is a time normally reserved for announcing good news.

But to his credit, Kerstetter followed through on an interview commitment made before his decision to resign.

In 1990, the bank would end up losing a stunning $85 million. Astounded shareholders wondered what, exactly, had become of their one-time worthwhile investment, while WSFS management and Associates tried to come to grips with how to proceed.

Lisa Brubaker, now executive vice president and chief information officer, was just beginning her career around that time, working at one of the bank branches.

"What I remember is that when I first started, the bank was very robust and growing very quickly. We were involved in a lot of things. You assumed the bank was doing very well because it was getting into all these ventures. The next thing you know, it was like, things fell downhill.

"It was like we went from riches to rags."

Chapter 4
Banking in His Blood

The tone in the room during the WSFS board meeting on January 23, 1990, must have been very somber. Mr. John F. Roche, deputy district director from the Office of Thrift Supervision, was delivering the results of a recent examination, and they didn't sound promising. By his count, WSFS faced a laundry list of growing financial concerns that were daunting both in number and severity. An excerpt from the meeting minutes shows just how bad things really were:

"[Mr. Roach's] report indicated that classified assets are too high, there has been a gradual erosion of capital, our service corporations are reporting negative earnings, the ratio of overdue loans to gross loans is 5.27%,[16] there appear to be credit quality problems…they believe our allowance for loan loss reserves is 'minimally adequate,' there are heavy concentrations in our loan portfolio, all of which will not be helped by the downturn in the local real estate conditions."

The final verdict from the examiners was an OTS composite rating of 3, which would require WSFS to enter into a second enforcement action with its regulator— a sequel to the one the bank had entered in late 1989.[17] This authorized the OTS to monitor the bank closely, and was ultimately intended to improve WSFS's financial health. It was a daunting sign for a financial institution that had spent the past several years investing heavily in growth— and in a yet-to-be-constructed $70 million, 30-story headquarters tower.

As the months marched on and the local real estate market continued to decline, the picture did not become any brighter for WSFS. Bewildered shareholders had their confidence shaken, and it would be logical to conclude that many of them wanted to jump out of the WSFS boat— as it seemed to be taking on significant quantities of water.

But at least one man was determined to stay on board. Actually, he wanted to be on *the* board— the board of directors. A year before he'd be frantically passing out investor booklets at the infamous June 19 meeting, CG Cheleden arrived on the WSFS scene. His gutsy commitment to the bank would ultimately become synonymous with WSFS' successful efforts to stay afloat and set sail for calmer waters. Here is his story.

Philadelphia, circa 1900. New immigrants, many of them Lithuanian, had arrived in the growing metropolis, forming tight-knit communities fed by a shared connection to the Old Country. As they found their footing in America, it was clear they'd need a safe place to keep their hard-earned savings— much like the conscientious Wilmingtonians had almost a century earlier.

The first Lithuanian Building and Loan Association in the area sprouted up on North Broad Street near City Hall. It was a quaint little bank, operated by people who still preferred to count and converse in their native slavic tongue rather than in English. Their aspirations were grounded: Just to raise enough money through deposits to be able to build a meetinghouse for themselves, and to help others in the neighborhood with their homes and businesses. Once a month, members of the association would meet in a local pub to put in another 10 or 25 cents, and someone would keep notes on who had contributed what.

In 1916, a young man named Charles Cheleden was invited to one of those meetings. Although he was just a 17-year-old high schooler, he'd already made an impression on his money-savvy elders. "Charlie, you're a smart boy," someone piped up. "You keep the books."

So he did, carrying the bank through the Great Depression: He'd go door-to-door on Fridays and Saturdays, collecting $5 here and there as loan payments; eventually convincing the adjacent bar owner not to withdraw his investment when the going got tough.

Four hundred other Buildings and Loans in Philadelphia failed, but the little community bank— by that point called Liberty Savings and Loan—survived. A few years later, Charles met Ann, the woman who would later become his wife. She was also no stranger to financial institutions: Family legend has it that she was so instrumental in the day-to-day running of a bank in South Philadelphia, it closed while she was off on her honeymoon. In 1943, the couple had a baby boy, who they named Charles George.

Some children have athletics in their blood; others have sciences or music. CG, as he came to be called by his friends, clearly had banking running through his veins. When he got a bit older, CG's mother started working at Liberty, too— heading up the advertising, marketing and promotion department. Her tactics to get townspeople to open new accounts included stroller parking for mothers with children and all sorts of unique giveaways: free calendars, hand-painted Japanese trays, and even bionic knives.

When CG was in high school, he worked Friday nights and summers at the bank. He started in the stock room, unloading and organizing his mother's stashes of promotional gifts; then moved on to man the bank's front door, letting people out before the 8 p.m. close and then running down to the accounting department to update the records for the day. Through those experiences, CG learned enough to be able to open accounts, and provided much-needed assistance as a teller on those busy payday evenings.

Meanwhile, hard-working Charles Cheleden had climbed the ranks, and was now leading the bank as CEO. "He was a guy who would stand in the lobby every day and watch how the customers were being served. He would engage them in Lithuaninan, see how they were being treated by the tellers," recalls CG of his father's extremely hands-on approach. And the dedication that Mr. and Mrs. Cheleden displayed in the office certainly didn't stop when they were at home. "They would talk banking over breakfast, lunch and dinner, and they wouldn't always agree," CG says with a laugh.

CG went on to study business and law at Villanova University, but summers at home meant he'd still go to work at the bank, opting to spend Friday nights behind the teller window instead of at the local watering hole with friends.

"In those days, nothing was on computers. There were ledger cards. They were used into the late 60s — early 70s. So they make a deposit, the teller pulls their card, they put it in a machine, enter the transaction, put their passbook in, and the machine would stamp both. So at the end of the day, I had a posting machine to make sure everything balanced out, with the cash and the deposits and the withdrawals, all that," he recalls.

As it turns out, the money he made at the bank—along with his very own passbook— would allow CG to make an all-important cash purchase: an engagement ring for his future wife, Noreen. The two had met in 1964, CG's senior year in college. By the time graduation came around, he was savvy enough to have risen to the top of his class— meaning that he'd be able to request placement right near her house for his mandatory tour of duty in the ROTC.

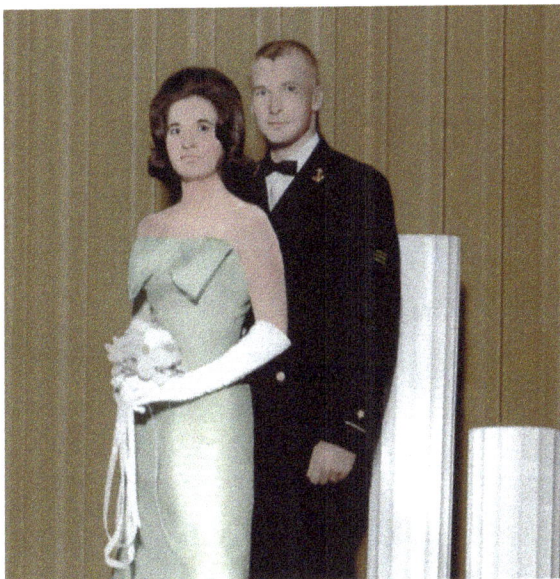

In 1967, CG finished up his Naval tour, married Noreen, and went back to work at the place that had always been home away from home: Liberty Savings and Loan. Always one to push the envelope in terms of ambition, he also enrolled in night classes at Temple Law School, where he was quick to chime in whenever the conversation turned to anything banking-related. While law had always been a passion of his, CG didn't want it to be his primary career— just a helpful asset to have in his back pocket. He was right.

By the time CG had passed the Bar exam in 1972, he was at the bank full-time, learning the mortgage trade from the ground up. "I was typing mortgage papers, chasing differences in the accounting department, calling delinquent borrowers, and reviewing appraisals," he remembers.

His father's insistence on transparency and communication enabled CG to develop strong relationships with the board members. "My dad wanted the board to know about the loans we were making, so once a month every board member would get a list of new loans. They would divide the list up and do a secondary inspection on these loans," CG recalls. "I'd take a board member out, and we'd look at five or six properties, for loans made the prior month, and the board members got to know me, I got to know them, we'd have lunch together. And if they didn't like the loan, they'd say at the next meeting, 'I think you're lending too much there.' So it kept the lenders on top of things, and it kept the board on top of things, and a few of the officers connected with the board."

After nearly a decade with the bank, 34-year-old CG had risen from corporate secretary to vice president. He felt ready for more, especially as he watched his father age into his 70s. If there was a perfect time for a promotion, this was it— at least, in his opinion.

"I go to his office, and I said 'Dad, I'm ready,'" he recalls, laughing. "So he made me president, he was chairman of the board, and he kept a good eye on me."

The same day that Jimmy Carter took his Oath of Office— January 20, 1977— the young Charles George was inaugurated as commander-in-chief of Liberty Savings and Loan. Mirroring Carter's middle-of-the-road approach to American politics, CG ran the bank conservatively, focusing on real-estate lending for homes and businesses along with some construction projects. As a result, the bank had very few bad loans.

By the early 1980s, Liberty had grown to about $250 million in assets. Riding the swelling tidal wave of financial deregulation coming from Congress at the time, CG took the bank public in 1984, joining an expanding list of Savings and Loans doing the same. He figured it would be a good way to grow the institution by raising capital, and to make some money off the stock. He was mostly right, but being a publicly-traded company came with plenty of additional headaches.

"It was a burden. We didn't have a really sophisticated management team, so we were scratching and clawing to keep up with the regulators and the shareholders, and Wall Street," CG recalls. The convoluted quarterly analyst meetings were certainly a far cry from the neighborhood pub meetups that CG's father had attended as a teen in the bank's early days. Charles Cheleden finally asked his son: "How are you going to get this monkey off your back?"

After carefully weighing the options, CG realized that his dad was right: Things were bound to get more and more complicated with Liberty as time rolled on, and he felt like he was destined to do other things, outside of the banking world. So, three years after going public, he decided to take advantage of the good market—and put the bank up for sale.

However, CG would soon learn that putting the bank "up for sale" was worlds away from actually "selling" the bank. A roller coaster ensued over the next few months, as prospective buyers came in and tried to finagle a deal with the no-nonsense descendant of Lithuanian immigrants.

Finally, a man named Alan Fellheimer—then the CEO of a bank holding company in Pittsburgh called Equimark—stepped up to the plate. After some negotiating, CG gave him the keys, and Fellheimer later made CG president of Equimark. Satisfied that he'd been able to step away from the stress of running a bank on his own, CG was happy in the role for a while, and he did make life a bit difficult for the Equimark lenders when he would point out problematic loans at board meetings. All was basically swimming along steadily— until Fellheimer let him go. "I frankly wasn't doing a whole lot, I was a figurehead, and the climate was changing, so he fired me," CG recalls. It was August, 1989.

Newfound unemployment didn't ruffle CG's feathers too much— he always had something cooking on the side. A few months earlier, while still employed at Equimark, he'd bought $400,000 worth of stock in a Delaware bank called the Wilmington Savings Fund Society, better known as WSFS. At that time, the shares were trading at $16; but by the end of the year, the bank announced a massive quarterly loss, and the price was down to single digits. It was not exactly the outcome he had expected.

With time on his hands, a significant portion of his net worth at stake, and experience in his back pocket, CG decided to get involved.

A David and Goliath Battle

WSFS had first appeared on CG's radar in the early 1970s, when the bank instituted its now-famous Plan Card. In fact, young CG was among the ranks of intrigued financial executives who visited from all over the world to learn about how the innovative program worked. As his career developed, the plucky Delaware savings and loan stuck in his mind. So, when it came time to look for a place to invest some of the money from the sale of Liberty, CG looked at WSFS stock. It appeared that Walt St. Clair might be close to retirement, and the market at the time was favorable for a likely sale of the bank — all signs that investors could realize a nice return on the bank's shares. He put in that $400,000.

But the increase in stock price was not to be for the Wilmington Savings Fund Society, and, by the fall of 1989, CG had seen his investment fall 50% over a period of six months. Clearly, serious trouble was brewing. Armed with the knowledge he had acquired from decades in the industry, alarmed at the tumbling value of WSFS shares, and newly free from other work obligations, CG took it upon himself to organize a meeting with Chairman and CEO Walt St. Clair.

"I called and asked if I could see him, and he gave me the courtesy of a visit to his office," CG recalled. While reaching out was bold enough to begin with, CG's next proposal would take his daring a step further. "I said 'you know, I have experience, I'd like to join your board.' Walt said 'no, basically, we don't need you.'"

St. Clair's rejection only served to light a fire under CG's determination. He soon realized that he had an ally: a friend named Bill Dimeling, who at that time owned 5% of WSFS stock. "Bill Dimeling— he was smart, he was an entrepreneur, and he was also a shark," CG remembers. "We decided we were going to try to rally some shareholders to join our cause and somehow get on the board."

Dimeling pushed CG to consult lawyers at a then-small Pittsburgh firm called Buchanan, Ingersoll & Rooney PC. If they were getting ready to fight, they might as well have weapons. The only problem: The opposing team had hired a firm called Skadden Arps, one of the largest firms in the country. It would be like trying to take down tanks with a bunch of bows and arrows.

"Skadden invites me up to New York to talk about this, and they keep me waiting in this big conference room," CG recalls. "This guy with big suspenders comes in, he's probably billing $1,500 an hour… and he said 'Son, the last person that tried to do this [stage a proxy fight], it cost them a million dollars and they lost.' Like, you're in over your head, don't even attempt it, you're nuts."

The Skadden, Arps lawyers weren't mincing their words when they said they would fight tooth and nail. When CG and his team requested a list of shareholders from the board so that they could start to solicit proxies— allowing shareholders to vote for board members other than the ones proposed by the company—they refused. CG and company went to court to force them to turn the list over. A full-blown David and Goliath-style proxy war was about to begin.

In the corporate world, a proxy statement is sent to shareholders along with the company's annual report. Shareholders are asked to sign the proxy indicating their support for decisions that are to be voted on at the annual meeting. Key amongst these is the selection of board members.

In the vast majority of situations, there is only one proxy sent to shareholders that comes from the company itself— so it was very unusual at the time for there to be a competing proxy that would be asking shareholders to vote for a different set of directors.

CG's proxy was the product of two months of diligent work, fueled by an intense desire to convince shareholders that WSFS needed a change in leadership. He would go to the Ingersoll office, sit down in the conference room, and type away. The associates would help him edit. Finally, by the beginning of 1990, he had a finished document that was ready to be filed with the SEC— a legal requirement, before it could be sent to shareholders. Spelling out 14 reasons why he and three other people of his choosing should be allowed to join the board, it was sure to make waves among WSFS bigwigs. The question was whether it would be enough to convince shareholders the same thing, especially at a time when proxy challenges were few and far between.

Those 14 reasons:

1. Earnings deteriorated in 1988 and there was a $5.8 million loss in 1989.
2. Problem loans increased from $12.9 million to $36.2 million in 1989.
3. The reserve for loan losses was woefully inadequate.
4. The stock price had lost over 50% in value in the last six months.
5. Operating expenses were out of line and out of control.
6. Management's assurance that matters were under control had not been borne out by the facts.
7. Management's poor judgement in deciding to build a new headquarters building.
8. Star States Development was a high risk venture that had also performed poorly.
9. Acquisition of Diversified Investment Group, Inc. was another questionable management judgement.
10. Star States' capital seemed dangerously close to going below the new regulatory minimums.
11. Management's resistance to the election of the committee's nominees was totally unjustified.
12. Management's resistance seemed like it could result in the wasteful expenditure of large sums of Start States' money.
13. The existing officers and directors of Start States owned only 5.3% of its stock.
14. Star States needed a new business plan.

In conclusion, CG emphasized that stockholders should send a clear message to management by electing the committee's four nominees.

Bracing for a firefight, CG was pleasantly surprised when the phone rang the day after he filed with the SEC, before he'd even sent the proxy out to shareholders. It was the top of the WSFS food chain— Walt St. Clair and Chief Operating Officer T.K. Kerstetter— asking him if they could talk things over. "So they realized they were probably going to lose four members on the board," recalls CG. His persuasive writing abilities and his impressive analysis, along with the leverage from Dimeling's status as a 5% shareholder, had defeated the giant— or at least brought him to the negotiating table. "So they sat down and they said 'we'll give you one.' I said 'One won't do it, I want at least two.' So they said 'who's it gonna be?'"

It was a major win for Team Cheleden, and relatively unheard-of, given the powerful (and expensive) forces he'd been up against: a legal lineup costing an estimated $400,000 versus the $10,000 he'd forked over for his effort. After consulting with Dimeling, CG chose Tom Preston, an upstanding Wilmingtonian (and a highly-respected prosecutor and attorney) to fill his second promised seat on the board. With that, the only other compromise he had to make was to not buy any more stock— a standstill agreement that would ensure that the newcomers wouldn't be able to take over the bank.

The New Kid on the Block

While scary for those at the top, the shake-up of the WSFS status quo undoubtedly provided a sliver of new optimism for the shareholders, who were unnerved by the bank's recent losses. "It was a new hope, a new light," CG recalls. But the shareholders were not the people he'd have to rub elbows with at monthly meetings. The other board members would certainly be eyeing this unlikely victor with suspicion; maybe even hostility.

At his first official board meeting on May 3, 1990— shortly after the WSFS annual meeting on April 25 where he and Tom had been elected— CG didn't contribute too significantly. "I didn't say a whole lot. I had received the board package with the examination report, and for the first time I saw that the examiners were coming down on their headquarters building, 'the hole in the ground', with a cease and desist order. That was all new matter to me, and they're putting up more reserves, they're off the budget— it was all chaos. So I was pretty much quiet, gathering info."

Aside from one board member who muttered a particularly snarky comment in CG's direction, the rest of the individuals in the boardroom regarded their new peers with a cold politeness. CG knew that they perceived him as a raider, with Tom as his sidekick, but all he could do was respond with warmth and a determination that his presence would ultimately help the bank. And, as that inaugural meeting would convey, the bank needed all the help it could get. First, the board officially suspended construction of the Star States Tower, which would be a huge blow to the bank's public image. Second, the board was informed of three class action lawsuits that had been filed, each alleging that for the period of January 1, 1989 through April 26, 1990, "the company did not fully and completely disclose commercial loan losses, etc. and violated Federal Security Laws which state that all material information regarding operations must be disclosed." If that weren't enough, members discussed the possible sale of various subsidiaries— and all on the heels of an April 26 action suspending the company's dividends.[18]

As spring turned to summer, it was obvious that things at the Wilmington bank continued to head downhill fast— so fast, in fact, that at every monthly board meeting, management was having to come up with new budget plans. Pressure was mounting on all sides: Pressure to solve the tower problem, scrutiny from regulators, negative press, and demands from investors. "By the time August came, I said 'We gotta do something,'" CG recalls.

But what, exactly, was he going to do? In CG's mind, the path forward involved a change in leadership. There was only one way to turn the tide in that direction, and it would require his most audacious move yet.

A Bid for the Throne

As he had done before, CG sat down at his word processor and began to write. It was one thing to try to get onto the board as an outsider; now, he was trying to advocate from the inside for a shake-up of top leadership. It was a difficult feat that could easily backfire: His fellow board members had approved many of the decisions that had become the sources of severe problems, and all of them had either been part of hiring the then-current leadership or had themselves been recruited to the board by Walt St. Clair. He could not be sure where their loyalties would lie. Despite the tide surging against him, CG felt strongly that the bank would not survive if things remained the way they were. So he drafted his argument and sent it around.

"I wrote all of them a two-page letter, Fed-Exed it to their houses, saying it's time for a change of management and we (the board) have to step up. Management had rose-colored glasses on, and we needed a fresh look, fresh approach to deal with the situation.

"I knew what I had to do, and I was determined to lay it out," he remembers.

The night before the August 1990 board meeting, the phone rang, much like it had several months ago after CG filed his proxy. Again, it was T.K. Kerstetter. "He said, 'Tomorrow, before the meeting, we'd like to convene, and have you and Tom [Preston] stay in the anteroom for a little while. We want to talk this over,'" CG recalls. "That was a good message that they were going to do something. They wanted time to think it over. They had seen the handwriting on the wall."

As T.K. remembers it: "I ended up calling Cheleden and Preston and saying, 'Listen, the biggest concern here now,' and I put Walt into this as well, I said, 'The biggest concern now is for the welfare of the bank. That's the responsibility, and if it means that there's a change of management, then let there be a change of management. It's clear to me that that's what the regulators [want] and what needs to happen now so that everything can move forward positively.'"

After discussing things with Kerstetter, Walt St. Clair decided to step down as the bank's CEO and president. For the second time in his involvement with WSFS, CG had prepared for a tough fight, only to be met with a somewhat easy path to victory. "This was an 11th-hour Hail Mary pass, and the timing could not have been any later," CG said.

Fortunately, it was successful, but now the stakes were much higher. At that very same meeting where St. Clair resigned, CG was asked to become Interim Chairman— a head-spinning transition for an outsider. In a matter of weeks, he'd become one of the most powerful players in the fight against the permanent closure of WSFS. But CG was confident that he had the credentials.

"I just took the seat at the head of the table, and we figured out who was going to be on the committee to find the new CEO," he remembers. "I had to wing it. They showed confidence in me... they threw the ball into my lap, and I had to run with it. I wasn't totally out of my element, it was just with a new set of players."

Tom Preston echoed the faith that many of his colleagues had in CG's ability to rise to the occasion. "My recollection is by the end of that very first meeting, nobody had any doubt that of all the people in that room, nobody knew more about banking than CG did, and most of us knew far, far less."

Never one for pomp and circumstance, CG was just ready to get to work. "I was determined if WSFS was viable that I was going to be part of it... I was happy that we had a path to the future."

A New Chapter Begins

As extraordinary and unusual as it was, CG's promotion was certainly not the end of troubles for WSFS. In fact, they were only intensifying: As 1990 progressed, the local real estate market continued to decline, darkening the prognosis for the bank's future. Increasingly plagued by deterioration in its commercial loan portfolio, WSFS declared a third-quarter loss of $17.6 million, and then a whopping fourth quarter loss of $37 million. By the time it was all totaled, 1990 would see a staggering $85.5 million of the bank's capital disappear. The company had started the year with a net worth of $90 million, but ended it with a net worth of less than $5 million. What a difference a year makes.

The dire situation made it crucial for WSFS to find a new CEO, and fast— but for the bank to have any hope of survival, it had to be the right person for the job.

[16] 5.27% is approximately 5 times what would be considered normal.

[17] This was a fair score out of a 5-level grading system, with 1 being the best rating. Grades 1 and 2 are considered passing while a 3 mandated additional supervision from the OTS. A 4 or 5 meant an institution was in serious jeopardy.

[18] WSFS board minutes from May 3, 1990.

Chapter 5
Star States Names a New CEO

With Walt St. Clair and T.K. Kerstetter out as top leadership, newly-minted Board Chairman CG Cheleden set up shop within WSFS to determine just how bad things were. He had to go from viewing things from 30,000 feet above, as any board member would do, to actually making management-level decisions as the acting CEO. That is quite a change for anyone, but this was literally overnight—he went from the frying pan into the fire.

"I was running the bank from an eye-level," CG recalls. "I'm talking to the lenders about this loan, that loan, this joint venture, you know, and then the hole in the ground and our poor OTS examination results, and none of it is good news, right. It felt like a sinking ship."

From CG's days working with Alan Fellheimer, he'd gotten to know of a woman named Pat Muldoon— an experienced loan workout specialist and manager. "She had an eye for spotting bad loans, and an aggressive, no-nonsense way of dealing with those borrowers that for whatever reason were unable to meet their loan repayment obligations," he recalls. As a dedicated "workout" person, Pat would fly across the country to help banks work out their nonperforming loans, determining which ones were worth saving: That is, deciding whether it made sense to work with the original borrower or foreclose on the loan. The hardest part of the job, of course, was confronting the desperate individuals or businesses that were in trouble, often through no fault of their own. But Pat's straight-and-narrow approach always got the job done.

CG felt that Pat was a natural to help save the sinking WSFS ship, and asked her to become a full-time Associate, rather than just a consultant. He put her in charge of the workout and recovery team that came to be known as SAM: the Special Asset Management Department. It would soon grow to more than a dozen people—more lenders than the bank had at the time. Pat would commute to Wilmington daily from her home in Philadelphia, and CG made a point of meeting with her every morning to review problem loans and investments and make decisions on what to do next.

By this point, it was becoming clear that CG had the skills to run WSFS, and some board members were certainly hoping for that outcome. But he wasn't on the same page. His early passion for law was coming back to him, and he had made a plan to open his own practice by the end of 1990. He also remembered how complicated things became with Liberty towards the end of his time there. "Frankly, I was tired of the regulations and the examiners and the bureaucratic stuff," he recalls. "When it came to me... I said, 'no, let's go on with the CEO search.'"

Speeding Up the Process

WSFS could not afford to take the time that most job searches take. The bank's back was against the wall, and CG knew he had to act fast. So, he devised a highly unusual strategy for screening candidates that would make the process move much faster. He had a 12-page case study about a struggling financial institution prepared. It was entitled XYZ Hypothetical Bank, but it was really a description of the mess at WSFS. It only took a few days. He then ran a simple 'Want' ad in the Wall Street Journal and American Banker.

In short order, about 120 resumes arrived. CG, the search committee members and a human resource professional reviewed them, deciding to send the case study to about half of the applicants. Of those, about 45 responses came back. The search committee quickly culled those down to about five or six of the most impressive individuals, and each of them was invited to Wilmington for a formal interview.

One of the last submissions came from an out-of-towner named Skip Schoenhals. His plan to save the bank quickly rose to the top of the pile.

"There was a great deal of discussion among the board about the need for someone local, who knew the markets," recalls then-Director Joe Julian, a member of the search committee. "But we agreed that the best paper came from some guy in Michigan. He laid out exactly what we needed to do."

Skip was given the final interview, and CG remembers that "he hit it out of the park." With no time to lose, the board made their decision.

Who exactly was this skilled new arrival from 800 miles away? The whole of WSFS was about to find out— and the bank would never be the same.

The Marvin 'Skip' Schoenhals Saga

In late summer of 1990, Skip Schoenhals was once again searching for a job: his third such search in as many years. Despite having a positive track record with two other problem thrifts in Michigan, a confluence of circumstances had created a difficult and uncertain period of time in the young banker's life. He describes this in depth in the 'Reflections' chapter at the end of this book. For now, let's pick up the story in August 1990, when he had just come off an unsuccessful bid to become the CEO of a $600 million bank in Wilkes-Barre, Pennsylvania.

Skip had been under heavy consideration to be the bank's new president. After several weeks and two separate trips to Wilkes-Barre, he was one of two finalists invited back for the deciding interview. In preparation, the headhunter had informed him that he was the company's top choice.

"I went into the final stage believing that I was the 'inside favorite,'" Skip remembers. "I was really excited, because it looked like my nearly 10-month search was nearing the end."

He didn't get the offer.

It turned out that the Pennsylvania bank was looking for someone who would be taking a step down from a larger institution; not someone working his way up the ladder. After nearly a year of trying to figure out his next move— and feeling like he'd finally found something solid— "it was a particularly demoralizing moment."

Star States Catches Skip's Eye

Barely a week after the stinging Pennsylvania rejection, Skip came across the interesting ad pictured above.

"I kind of knew where Delaware was because I went to Wharton in Philadelphia for my MBA, but Star States in Delaware—who's ever heard of that? I almost missed it, but once I figured out it was a bank holding company, I sent my resume in," he recalls.

Not long after that, Skip received a big envelope in the mail: the bank wanted him to respond to the case study. He was excited enough that he opened the envelope while still standing at his mailbox, out in front of the house. Walking back to the yard, he started to scan its contents. He quickly realized that XYZ Hypothetical Bank was more than double the size of the Wilkes-Barre bank.

"I looked at it and it was a billion-and-a-half-dollar bank. I had just been put out on my butt because I wasn't good enough for a $600 million bank," he recalls. Still reeling from that rejection, he remembers thinking, "why bother to complete the case study?" If Skip was too small-time for Wilkes-Barre, how would he ever cut it at WSFS, over twice the size?

Luckily, some words of wisdom from his wife changed his mind.

"Linda, in one of those just wonderful and clarifying, what I call fog-cutter questions, said, 'Skip, if they called you up for an interview, would you go?' I said, 'Well, of course I'd go.' She then asked, 'Would you prepare for the interview, do some homework?' I said, 'Of course I would.' She then said, 'Then why don't you look at this as preparation for the interview?' The question completely changed my perspective."

"I don't know if, left to my own devices, I would have ever picked up the case study again or not—doesn't matter—but I came close to throwing it in the trash bin. My wife saved me from it."

Skip got to work on the study, but he was up against a one-week deadline. After an intense few days of writing, editing and revising, he managed to crank out his proposal, with the help of the sluggish word processors of that era. He remembers making the last few edits with the FedEx guy in his driveway, waiting on each precious page to slowly come out of the typewriter-like printer. It took forever.

The stress was worth it. Skip's submission made it to Wilmington in the nick of time. Furthermore, the case method played on two of his biggest strengths: He was adept at analyzing problems, and could eloquently express his ideas in writing. He came up with a plan to lead the bank to solvency, with the most crucial step being an aggressive plan to deal with problem loans and real estate investments. He also outlined the importance of restoring appropriate relationships with the regulatory agencies, and detailed a few other courses of action— including plans to sell WSFS' real estate brokerage subsidiary, the B. Gary Scott Company, and additional non-strategic assets.

Skip was scheduled to go to Washington, D.C. for another interview, so he was able to combine that trip with his WSFS visit. The following day, he hopped on the train for the short ride from Washington to Wilmington. While Skip doesn't remember much about his first arrival in the city, a funny recollection remains ingrained in his mind: Heading out to the bank the next morning, he started up a conversation with his hotel's fresh-faced manager, who asked where he was off to. When Skip told the young man that he was in town for an interview at WSFS, he was met with a blank stare, followed by a question: "What is WSFS? A radio station?"

Skip was struck by the manager's cluelessness— wasn't WSFS supposed to be a well-known local institution? He wondered what he was getting himself into. (Skip only learned later that the hotel manager had been in town for merely a week, so was at a slight disadvantage).

Radio station or not, Skip's visit proved fruitful: Much as the case study showcased Skip's skills, his interview with the WSFS team did, too. Despite being in what many people would consider a nightmarish format— four members of the search committee, each firing questions on a range of subjects— Skip thrived. It was a true test of his ability to stay on his toes and seamlessly jump from one topic to another. "I've had several group interviews in my lifetime and they've always gone really well," Skip recalls. "This was set up to align with strengths that I already had."

After another afternoon meeting with an additional member of the search committee and an early dinner at a local Wilmington restaurant, Skip returned to West Bloomfield, Michigan. The next few weeks are a bit of a blur, but he recalls a few phone conversations with CG and another in-person meeting with him at WSFS to discuss what the terms of employment would be.

Around the 10th of October, Skip was officially offered a position as the CEO of WSFS. He accepted, of course. He was relieved, but there were also a few other thoughts swirling around in his mind. Taking the job would mean that he and Linda would have to leave their home in Michigan, which was something they hadn't really wished to do. What would life in Wilmington be like? Besides some apprehension about the relocation, Skip recognized that there was a lot riding on his ability to save the troubled bank. At least his job search was over, but would he have what it would take to set WSFS straight?

Hoping for relief, Star States hires consultant

By PETER OSBORNE
Staff reporter

WILMINGTON — Star States Corp., parent company of Wilmington Savings Fund Society and B. Gary Scott Realtors, is expected to announce Wednesday that it has hired a Michigan banker to reverse its recent financial slide.

A Star States spokeswoman said the beleaguered holding company has hired Marvin N. "Skip" Schoenhals, 43, as a consultant. She would not say he will assume the president and chief executive officer positions left vacant by the resignations Aug. 3 of J. Walton St. Clair Jr. and Thomas K. Kerstetter.

Sources said Star States is waiting for the federal Office of Thrift Supervision to approve Schoenhals' appointment and might package his hiring announcement with the release of third-quarter earnings on Wednesday.

Schoenhals most recently was president and chief executive officer of Peoples Savings Bank in Monroe, Mich. He left in January after it was acquired by Standard Federal Bank of Troy, Mich., the state's second largest thrift, with $9.6 billion in assets.

Schoenhals was hired by Peoples, a $380 million (assets) thrift, after regulators began investigating the thrift for possible violations of securities laws connected to its 1987 initial stock offering.

Schoenhals restated the bank's financial statements for the previous three years, retained a new accounting firm, improved loan controls and replaced some personnel. During his time with Peoples, delinquent loans were reduced by 75 percent to $1.5 million, charge offs were reduced by 81 percent, and net income jumped 60 percent, to $2.4 million.

When he joined Peoples, the stock was trading in the $8 range. About six months later, he negotiated the merger agreement for an eventual price of $18.65 per share.

The resignations of St. Clair and Kerstetter came following a $26.6 million second-quarter loss.

The $1.6 billion (assets) thrift, which is addressing its real estate portfolio problems under the scrutiny of federal regulators, lost $3.7 million in the first quarter and eliminated its quarterly dividend. Just over a year ago, the company's stock was selling for $14.13 per share. It closed Friday at $2.

Luckily, he'd have some time to get his feet wet before wading into the deep end. Since WSFS was still under a 'Regulatory Order,' Skip's hiring as CEO had to be approved by the OTS. While he waited for that to go through, he got settled in Wilmington and began to work at the bank as a consultant, so that he could get his bearings and hit the ground running once he was given the green light.

The OTS blessed Skip's hiring during the last week of October, so November 1, 1990, was his first official day in the new role.

The best part? Thanks to CG's genius— if unconventional— hiring strategy, Skip already had a plan in mind for steering the bank out of troubled waters. He was ready to get started.

91

Chapter 6
Skip Gets to Work

Turning WSFS around was not going to be accomplished overnight. The details of Skip's first days on the job are blurry now, but this interview with News Journal reporter Peter Osborne on the following pages gave insiders and outsiders a glimpse of what the bank's new leader was thinking.

The core values Skip discussed with Peter— patience, perseverance, integrity and straight-forward thinking— were the pillars that he'd use to uphold WSFS for the next two decades. But in November of 1990, Skip still had a lot to prove. With no time to waste, he rolled up his sleeves and focused on turning his hypothetical case study plan into a reality that could save the beleaguered Wilmington institution. Before anything else, Skip knew that he'd have to identify the asset quality and capital problems left in the wake of the bank's expansion into new kinds of lending and investing in the late 1980s.

"Outside of the hole in the ground [for the headquarters], which was a unique situation, problem banks are all about bad credit. It's easy to grow a bank when you're lending the money. When it's time to get it to come back, that's when you discover, whoa, that it didn't work the way you thought it would," he recalls. "This is especially true when an organization rapidly increases lending in an area in which it had limited experience. In addition to the loans, the bank also had entered into various partnerships to directly develop residential real estate projects, and those too required objective review."

Marvin N. Schoenhals

Title: President, Chief Executive Officer, Star States Corp.

Age: 43

Family: Married, 8-year-old daughter

Education: BBA, University of Michigan, 1969
MBA, University of Pennsylvania, 1971

Hometown: Kalamazoo, Mich.

Activities:
Mayor, Owosso, Mich.
Chairman, Livingston County (Mich.) United Way campaign
President, Rotary Club of Owosso

Hobbies: Woodworking, cooking, reading

Strengths: "My ability to recognize problems and define plans; to create a vision and get people to work toward that"

Weaknesses: "Sometimes I get bored with routine."

Dealing with mad shareholders: "Every single person wants what we want: to return Star States to its former standing. When presented with a good plan and track record, shareholders will support what we're doing."

"Sometimes I get bored with routine."

News Journal

New Star States CEO seeks Disney magic

By PETER OSBORNE
Staff reporter

WILMINGTON — It's a bit disconcerting to hear a banker respond

"We must deal with the mistakes and go back to the heritage of being a class act. But it will require patience to work through the problems."

Schoenhals says it's too early to of-

Full article is reprinted in the Appendix, page 193.

plans.

Star States's stock price over the last year has dropped from a high of $14.13 to about $2, where it's hovered for about a week.

Schoenhals says he's here for the duration, despite a resume that paints the picture of a turn-around specialist who leaves when the job is complete.

"My aspiration is not to be a wanderer," he says. "I want to deal with the short-term problems and then move on to build an organization that everyone is proud of.

"My job is to fix the problems and provide leadership. Doing that will create shareholder value. I'm not charged with getting the bank ready for sale. I hope we perform so well that our stockholders won't want to sell."

Michigan bankers who have followed Schoenhals' career say they'll believe that when they see it.

"He's a troubleshooter, and a good one," said one banker during last week's American Bankers Convention. "He engineered the sale of Peoples under fairly lucrative terms and it was a fiasco when he arrived. He's forthright and low-key, one of the most unbanklike people I've ever met."

Schoenhals left his job as president and chief executive officer of $380 million (assets) Peoples Savings Bank in Monroe, Mich., in January after it merged with the much larger Standard Federal Bank of Troy, Mich.

When Schoenhals arrived at Peoples in 1988, the bank was being investigated by the Federal Home Loan Bank Board for possible violations of securities laws. Shortly after going public, Peoples reported significant losses from problems in its consumer loan portfolio.

Within months, Schoenhals had restated the bank's financial statements for the previous years, hired a new accounting firm, improved loan controls and replaced some personnel. The result? Delinquent loans were reduced by 75 percent to $1.5 million, charge-offs dropped 81 percent and net income jumped 60 percent to $2.4 million.

"Peoples' problems were about what I expected," Schoenhals says. "My charge was to fix the bank; no sale was contemplated. We ultimately looked at the bank's future and asked if we should consider a sale. We decided that if we were offered $18 per share, we probably had to let the shareholders vote."

Standard Federal paid $18.65 per share; when Schoenhals took over, the stock was selling for $8.

Schoenhals has spent his career eliminating problems. While some say "he gets rid of non-performing loans and non-performing people," Schoenhals prefers to say he's "an excellent leader who is hard on problems and works with people."

Thomas Cantalini, a Florida bank consultant who has been Schoenhals' chief financial officer in two turnaround situations, describes his former boss as "very methodical and thoughtful.

He lets you know what's expected but gives you time to do it. He's not the type to start letting the people go [when he arrives], but he picks up pretty quickly who the performers and non-performers are."

Schoenhals' resume includes a 13-year stint with increasingly responsible positions at Grand Rapids, Mich.-based Old Kent Financial Corp., leaving the well-respected bank holding company as a senior vice president at its lead bank.

"As a manager, I guess I'm a blend between cheerleading and quiet leadership," he said. "All the cheerleading you do will fall on deaf ears if the substance isn't there. You can't be a chief executive officer and stay in your office all day. But I won't be someone who goes and parties with the staff, either."

Schoenhals says he can bring a new perspective to the problems at Star States. Discussion of corporate strategy mirrors what St. Clair and Kerstetter were saying until their departure: re-emphasize the core banking business and concentrate commercial lending on small businesses.

Of course, federal regulators have already dictated that approach. But those who know Schoenhals said the banker understands the juggling act necessary at Star States.

"He knows how to keep his eye on the ball," said attorney Eugene Driker of the Detroit law firm of Barris, Sott, Denn & Driker. "He knows how to keep the institution humming and still negotiate through the waves and bring the boat to shore.

"Many businessmen are linear thinkers -- lining up the problems single file and then dealing with them. Not Skip. He understands the interrelationship between problems."

Says former Peoples Chairman Robert Scott: 'His rapport with regulators is unbelievable..He's a straight-shooter."

He says he used to be a workaholic; now he's "an effective manager and leader [who] balances what he does."

Asked what he hopes others will say about him, Schoenhals paused before answering:

"That I am a fair and competent husband, father and manager. And that my relationship with God came first."

Full article is reprinted in the Appendix, page 194.

For example, Skip found a Wilmington restaurant loan of approximately $6 million: So unrealistic that in order for it to pay off as planned, the sales would have had to reach unheard-of levels for a Wilmington restaurant at the time. There was also a residential condominium joint venture development of approximately $12 million: A perfect example of the adage that one partner had the money (WSFS) and the other (the developer) had the experience. When it was over, however, WSFS had the experience and the developer had the money— or at least some of it. That project would eventually cost the bank approximately $8 million to resolve.

"As the new CEO, you want to draw a line in the sand between your decisions and the previous management's decisions. This is especially true with loan valuations. A new CEO has to take off the rose colored glasses that can impact those who made the original decisions, and is uniquely positioned to do that— they have no ties to the past, so they can be as objective as possible," Skip explained.

To help with a valuation assessment, Skip brought in a team from the Regulatory Advisory Services Group of Price Waterhouse: now PricewaterhouseCoopers (PwC). They had a major job ahead. The goal was a thorough review of 75% of the bank's commercial loan-related portfolio.

At the start of the project, which would take until mid-December to produce preliminary conclusions, Skip addressed the PwC group.

"Guys, there are three possible outcomes to the work you are starting," he remembers telling them. "One, we get the valuations absolutely right; two, the valuations are still too optimistic; or three, the valuations turn out to be too conservative resulting in 'over-reserving' the bank. Of those three outcomes, I'd rather it be the last one, I'd rather be so conservative that we've underestimated the values."

While the mid-December completion date was reasonable for the scope of the study, it created awkward timing for WSFS given the existential threat looming on the immediate horizon: The bank was due for an exam in late November by the Office of Thrift Supervision, its primary regulator. So, with the valuation project under way, Skip approached the OTS. He knew that the regulators' primary focus would be on loan valuations, and if they found that those valuations were too rosy, the whole of the stately Wilmington institution would likely be forced to shut its doors forever.

"I said to them, 'I'd like to ask you to wait. I just got here. I'm starting this study of asset quality. As soon as it's done I'll give you complete access to it. You can use it as a starting point for your exam,'" Skip remembers.

His trustworthy track record with two other problem thrifts in Michigan meant that Skip had a good relationship with regulators: particularly with John Downy, the Director of Safety and Soundness at the OTS. As it turns out, Skip had worked with him when Mr. Downey had been the regional supervisor of thrifts in the midwest, before he'd been promoted to the director position. During Mr. Downey's tenure in the Midwest, Skip had been hired to resolve two different problem thrifts, leading to a history of mutual respect between the two men. So, when Skip came around with his all-important entreaty, Mr. Downey was inclined to hear him out.

"I don't know how much deliberation occurred over the request, but they did reschedule the exam for February," Skip recalls. "That's very, very significant in the story. As the PwC work would eventually conclude, if they'd come in November they would've found the bank under-reserved for its problem loans. That would have said management hasn't recognized the problems, hasn't dealt with them, and they usually had one solution when they discovered that condition: the bank gets sold or closed almost immediately. By delaying the exam, they gave us a chance to get our arms wrapped around it."

It was one small victory, to be sure, but the bank had storms yet to weather: The valuation project by PwC, although ultimately beneficial, would have a disastrous consequence in the short term. Skip's instructions to the PwC team to be 'conservative' was a catch-22 that almost went too far.

Bad Press: Customers Panic, Associates Sweat

By the end of December, the PwC work led to the preliminary conclusion that WSFS would have to charge off between $13 million and $24 million. That definitely was not a great sign, especially after substantial additions to the loan loss reserve and other charge-offs in the previous four quarters. One of the most shocking write-downs involved the acquisition of Fidelity Federal Savings and Loan Association: WSFS had paid $24.4 million for it when the transaction had finally closed in February of 1990, but when PwC was done with its analysis, it became clear that the bank had overpaid by $9.5 million.

That bad decision and many more like it were the reason that WSFS was now fighting for its life, but another major tidal wave was on the way.

As a public company, WSFS had a duty to disclose any significant anticipated losses to shareholders as soon as they became known. Therefore, with the knowledge of those major fourth-quarter deficits on the horizon, the bank had no choice but to make an immediate announcement. On December 21, a Friday afternoon (when most public companies release bad news, because fewer people read the Saturday paper) WSFS issued a press release detailing what was to come.

Skip had gone home to Michigan for the weekend to spend time with his family, who had not yet moved to Wilmington. As he sipped his coffee in bed on Saturday morning, the phone rang. It was one of his assistants with dire news: WSFS was making headlines all over the city, and it wasn't pretty. "$28 Million Loss Rocks Star States," cried the Wilmington *News Journal*. "WSFS parent concerned S&L may be in jeopardy."

$28 million loss rocks Star States
WSFS parent concerned S&L may be in jeopardy

By PETER OSBORNE
Staff reporter

WILMINGTON — The parent company of Wilmington Savings Fund Society said Friday it will lose up to $28 million in the fourth quarter and expressed concern over the thrift's ability to weather continued softness in local real estate markets.

Star States Corp. President Marvin N. Schoenhals said the thrift's future will be determined "over the next six to 12 months."

"We've identified our known problems," he said. "But if the real estate market gets a lot worse, we're going to have more problems."

The hefty fourth-quarter loss means Star States, which also owns B. Gary Scott Realtors, will lose between $70 million and $76 million — $14.58 to $15.83 per share — in 1990.

"I'm still convinced that this company will survive," Schoenhals said Friday afternoon. "We're concentrating on identifying all of our known problems, and we've done that at this point.

"There is no indication that Star States is a target of the regulators. I believe [the federal Office

of Thrift Supervision] is committed to working with the new management to allow [it] the opportunity to deal with the problems created by prior decisions."

Schoenhals said Star States will add between $12 million and $18 million to its loan-loss reserve, write down the value of intangible assets by $8.5 million, and settle a class-action lawsuit, paying $725,000 to stockholders who bought, sold or held Star States shares between Jan. 1, 1989, and July 17, 1990.

SCHOENHALS

The sizable addition to the loan-loss reserve, which stood at $21 million in late October, came after a review of the thrift's loan portfolios and related assets by the Regulatory Advisory Services Group of the Price Waterhouse accounting firm.

Trading in the company's stock was halted for about 90 minutes before and after the midafternoon announcement. Trading resumed about 45 minutes before the market closed.

See STAR STATES — A7

FROM PAGE A1

ket closed.

Star States closed at $1.875 per share, unchanged from Thursday's close.

Schoenhals was named president and chief executive officer of Star States and WSFS in November, three months after the resignations of Chairman and CEO J. Walton St. Clair Jr. and President Thomas K. Kerstetter amid disclosure of a $26.6 million second-quarter loss.

Schoenhals said the cost-cutting measures being taken "are not likely to include across-the-board cuts in staffing or reductions in service levels. The subject of additional branch consolidations is under review."

Star States has filed an amended capital plan that lays out how it plans to meet increasingly harsh federal capital requirements. Schoenhals wouldn't discuss the particulars of the plan but predicted Star States will shrink to about $1 billion in assets from its current $1.5 billion over the next few years.

Those familiar with the company rate the thrift's future as a tossup between remaining independent, merging with a large

commercial bank or being taken over by regulators.

Under any of those scenarios, shareholder deposits up to $100,000 would continue to be insured by the Federal Deposit Insurance Corp.

Although it will hurt fourth-quarter earnings, devaluing the intangible assets will boost long-term profitability, Schoenhals and local brokers said. On Sept. 30, intangible assets totalled $16.1 million.

Star States has been evaluating the future economic benefits from the $10 million in goodwill resulting from its acquisition of Fidelity Federal Savings and Loan Association last February.

Goodwill — generally understood to represent the value of a respected business name or good customer relations — has no independent market or liquidation value and must be written off over a period of time, 15 years in this case.

Schoenhals conceded Friday that the acquisition "was not a good one for Star States," but quickly added that his assessment has the benefit of hindsight.

"We know a lot more today about Fidelity than we knew about them on the day of the acquisition," Schoenhals said. "Because of the growth restriction placed on us by regulators and the increasing deterioration in the real estate markets, what was a good loan then is not worth much today."

As a result of writing down the value of those assets, Star States will add between $700,000 and $1 million to its bottom line each year, beginning in 1991.

Schoenhals also said the thrift was not acknowledging its guilt in the shareholder suit but settled because "to defend the lawsuit would cost a lot of money and time" that could be better spent on other things.

The company's largest shareholder, Wilmington entrepreneur John Rollins Sr., said that while he hopes the problems are worked out, he's not responsible for the company's increasingly aggressive posture toward addressing the problems in its real estate portfolio.

"We're not going to sweep our problems under the table," Schoenhals said. "Here's the dirty laundry; now we're going ahead."

Full article is reprinted in the Appendix, page 198.

As Skip's assistant read him the article, he quickly realized that going home for the weekend had probably been a mistake. "I shouldn't have been surprised, but 'oh my gosh, this much attention," he recalls thinking. He braced himself for the fallout, but that first piece of bad press mostly just rattled some nerves.

Still, nerves were rattled enough that on January 16, 1991, the *News Journal* ran a story with the headline, "WSFS not closing, regulator says." Apparently, *News Journal* business reporter Peter Osborne had contacted the OTS, WSFS' primary regulator. While a regulator normally will not make any comments about a particular bank, there had been enough "chatter" that William C. Eayre, Assistant Director of the OTS, responded to Peter with several colorful quotes. The full article is reproduced below, but here are some highlights:

- "Rumors that WSFS soon will be shut down by regulators are 'absolutely baseless.'"
- "Whoever is starting these rumors is just flat out wrong and is creating a lot of mischief and a lot of heartache."

WSFS not closing, regulator says

Flood of phone calls prompts comment

By PETER OSBORNE
Staff reporter

WILMINGTON — A high-ranking federal regulator on Tuesday broke a long-standing policy against commenting on individual thrifts by describing as "absolutely baseless" rumors that Wilmington Savings Fund Society soon will be shut down by regulators.

In the past week, nearly $10 million in insured deposits have been withdrawn by nervous customers.

"WSFS is not being closed down and is not on any list to be closed down," said William C. Eayre, assistant director of the Office of Thrift Supervision's Pittsburgh office.

The comment is unusual in that it runs counter to a long-standing OTS policy against commenting on specific institutions under regulatory supervision. But a flood of customer questions to the thrift, regulators and media in recent days led regulators and WSFS management to fight back Tuesday.

Eayre said that while the troubled thrift is not yet out of the woods, it is taking steps to work out its problems. He added that while no regulator will make predictions about future actions, rumors of an impending closing are

untrue.

"We normally don't comment on where individual institutions stand, but this is an absolutely baseless rumor," Eayre said. "We've been getting lots of phone calls from concerned customers. Whoever is starting these rumors is just flat wrong and is creating a lot of mischief and a lot of heartache."

Marvin N. Schoenhals, president and chief executive officer of WSFS parent Star States Corp., said the thrift received more than 100 phone calls from concerned customers asking about the rumors. But he said he was especially disturbed that some customers cashed in their certificates of de-

posit early, paying an interest penalty. The nearly $10 million in deposits withdrawn from customer accounts represents less than 1 percent of WSFS's deposit base. Schoenhals said the withdrawals are coming from accounts that are covered by the Federal Deposit Insurance Corp.

Schoenhals said he was offering an amnesty program to depositors who were misled by the rumor mill.

"It's frustrating to me to see people sacrificing their money in this way," Schoenhals said. "We'll refund the interest penalty and reinstate the original rates to anyone who redeposits those CDs by the close of business next Tuesday."

Full article is reprinted in the Appendix, page 202.

Mr. Eayre didn't know it, but another shoe was about to drop. As discussed, the early conclusions from the PwC work had led to that December announcement. But upon further analysis, it was decided that the final charge-off number would have to be at the higher end of the range; by the time all was said and done, it was clear the number would be so high that it would be out of that range altogether.

So, on January 26, 1991, another cold Saturday morning, the Wilmington *News Journal* once again hit shelves around town. This time, the headline was truly startling: "Star States posts $37 million loss."

Thirty-seven million dollars: That's how much WSFS ended up losing in the fourth quarter and having to divulge to the public when PwC finally finished tallying up all of those loan charge-offs. It was another catastrophic revelation from a bank that had lost almost its entire net worth over the course of 1990: After starting the year with $90 million in capital, $85 million had disappeared. There are very few companies that have ever lost 94% of their net worth in only a year, and even fewer that have lived to tell the story.

Star States posts $37 million loss

By PETER OSBORNE
Staff reporter

WILMINGTON — The housecleaning at Star States Corp. is under way in earnest.

The parent company of Wilmington Savings Fund Society and B. Gary Scott Realtors on Friday reported a $37.7 million loss for the fourth quarter, completing a dismal year that included setting aside $33.3 million for potential and actual loan losses.

The company reported a loss of $85.5 million, or $18.01 a share, for the year. Star States also said it would lease its Star States Tower site property on Rodney Square to Wilmington developer Ernest F. Delle Donne, and had completed the sale of its Anderson Leasing subsidiary and other real estate assets.

President and Chief Executive Officer Marvin N. Schoenhals said the actions, combined with future asset sales, should allow the company to be profitable this year, unless the economy continues its tailspin.

"We believe all the problems are on the table; the unknowns are the economy and how our customers react," said Schoenhals, adding that he is continuing to focus on strengthening the company's core retail banking business.

The results announced Friday will come as little surprise to investors and customers since Star States management has been openly discussing its problems and even predicted a large loss in late December.

Star States stock closed Friday at 2⅛, up ⅜. The loss was reported in mid-afternoon.

The $16.2 million addition to loan-loss reserves in the fourth quarter, along with the goodwill writedowns, came after a review of the thrift's loan portfolios and related assets by the Regulatory Advisory Group of the Price Waterhouse accounting firm.

Although Star States had predicted it would lose up to $28 million in the fourth quarter, the additional loss was primarily due to devaluing its intangible assets by $5.7 million more than it planned in December.

Better known as goodwill, intangible assets generally understood to represent the value of a respected business name or good customer relations have no independent market or liquidation value and must be written off over a period of time, 15 years in this case.

With its decision to write down the $16.3 million in goodwill and assets accounting for more than 40 percent of the fourth quarter loss — Star States has now completely eliminated its goodwill.

Schoenhals said 1991 will be spent continuing the restructuring of operations. The primary subsidiary, WSFS, falls far short of complying with all three federal capital requirements.

Schoenhals said one way of improving capital is through the sale of assets, but did not elaborate beyond saying Star States would sell a 58,000-square-foot site at 10th and Jefferson streets in downtown Wilmington to Delle Donne.

He also said Star States has entered into "an agreement in principle" to consolidate WSFS operations into a single 60,000- to 80,000-square-foot downtown site in 1992. He declined to say where that consolidation would take place but said the company's operations center on Philadelphia Pike would not be affected.

Federal regulators, to combat persistent rumors, recently took the unusual step of saying they had not targeted WSFS for closure.

Full article is reprinted in the Appendix, page 204.

Home Sweet.... Home?

As this news hit, Skip and Linda were settling into their new house in Wilmington— trying to remain hopeful, despite the grim reports.

"When the headline came out, it gave me a momentary pause," Linda remembers. "I was thinking, 'are we staring into the abyss?' But that didn't last long. I thought if anyone can do it, it's Skip. And I know he's doing all the right things, so we just soldiered on."

While the Schoenhals were sad to leave their family behind in Michigan, Wilmington represented important opportunities for Skip. As Linda put it: "Skip needs a challenge. He wakes up every morning and thinks 'what can I conquer today?' And he wasn't conquering anything over there."

For her part, Linda was happy to break free of the cold, gray Michigan winters. Though the hypothetical skies above WSFS were darkened by uncertainty, she felt confident that Skip could bring sunny days back again.

"I had been a banker too, so I understood what was going on and what it would take. Beyond that one momentary pause, I knew he could do it."

Colliding Crises

Sure, $37 million was an astonishing figure for an institution of WSFS's size. It would have attracted attention in the best of times. But things were far from normal for financial institutions during this period— there were other forces at play outside of WSFS' control.

Throughout 1989 and 1990, a "rolling" bank crisis had unfolded across the country, resulting in a steady stream of headlines about banks being closed by regulators. By mid-January of 1991, there were two particular situations receiving national attention. One involved the Bank of New England, a large institution headquartered in the Northeast. Its troubles were aired consistently over the nightly news for several weeks, complete with pictures of terrified people lining up outside local branches to get their money out before their bank failed. The other big issue of the moment was unfolding in New Hampshire, where the larger banking calamity gripping the U.S. was leading to a collapse of state-chartered credit unions. Since those institutions had deposit insurance through a state agency, not the FDIC, citizens worried that New Hampshire would run out of funds to reimburse their losses.

With all of that as a backdrop, WSFS' grim announcement turned into a full-blown calamity. By Monday morning, the WSFS team became concerned about the possibility of a 'run on the bank:' a Hollywood-like scene where people would line up to withdraw their deposits. Ultimately, there was a 'mini-run' a week or so later, with customers taking out $100 million in deposits— a tremendous sum for a bank of WSFS' size[19].

In an effort to quell the widespread panic, management decided to put senior officers in every branch for that week. "We wanted to reassure depositors as well as bank Associates that WSFS had the resources to weather the storm," Skip recalls.

He spent three days at a local branch, so that he could talk to people as they came in to withdraw: Maybe hearing encouraging words straight from the horse's mouth could convince Wilmingtonians to keep their confidence in the bank.

On one of those days, Skip noticed that it was mostly older people coming in— perhaps they still harbored terrifying recollections of hardship and loss following the bank closures of the early 1930s. His interaction with one such couple remains ingrained in his memory to this day:

"It was clear from the condition of their eyes and faces and their anxiety that they hadn't slept. I asked them why they were there, and they said, 'We're concerned about our money. We remember the Depression. We remember banks being closed. We're here to close our accounts.'"

"I had what I thought was a very logical conversation: 'Your money's safe. It's FDIC-insured.' They seemed to be reassured by that."

When they had finished talking, Skip moved on to speak with other people, and watched out of the corner of his eye as the couple walked up to the teller window.

"After they'd left, I went up to the teller and I said, 'What did those people do?' The teller said, 'They closed their account.'"

So much for his persuasive abilities. The next question Skip asked: "How much was in their account?"

"Sixty-one hundred dollars."

That would have been small potatoes for FDIC insurance, which covered savings of up to $100,000 at the time. But such reasoning meant little to people who had been through the likes of the Great Depression. They wanted their money in hand, immediately.

"That really struck me," Skip recalls. " I can remember the look on their faces to this day, and it just gives me an appreciation for the impact of the anxiety and panic they felt."

Unfortunately, the widespread uncertainty didn't end with customers; WSFS Associates also became caught up in the roller coaster of that week.

Then-Associate Cheryl Hughes, now the senior vice president and director of operations & application support, recalls the surreal experience of working with a team of management to coordinate strategic placement of armored cars throughout the state, in anticipation of a real-life run on the bank (just as Chip Clifton had in the late 1980s.)

Robin Williams, senior vice president of consumer banking at the time, remembers people lining up outside WSFS branches before 9 a.m., waiting for the bank to open so that they could withdraw. The sight of the gathering crowd would play on the nerves of other customers, convincing them to do the same.

"The viral situation hit some of the branches in a pretty dramatic way. There was one branch that closed one afternoon with $200 in cash left," Williams recalls. She got her own father to change his $20,000 of Krugerrands gold coins into cash, so that she would have enough money to deliver to clients. "That was one day that I was particularly in a sweat."

Thankfully, WSFS Associates never did have to dip into those undercover stockpiles of cash— the withdrawals did not escalate to such cinematic proportions. But living through this tumultuous episode in the bank's history certainly gave Associates their fair share of grit, as well as a fierce dedication to Wilmington's resilient old thrift.

Lisa Brubaker, who was then the director of retail strategy, sums it up well. "I do remember even back then feeling upset by customers who were worried about the safety of their money in the bank. I remember feeling that sort of ownership of, 'Well, of course the bank's going to take care of you, and why would you doubt that your money would be safe?'

"I had that affinity back then with the bank in terms of wanting it to survive and not wanting customers to feel like it couldn't be trusted."

Fortunately, the dramatic cash outflow stemmed by the end of that scary week. Had it not, the bank could have eventually hit a liquidity crisis that would likely have forced it into the arms of the FDIC: a certain death.

[19] Fortunately, it was a 'quiet mini-run:' Had it become well-known, the outcome might have been different. More on this later.

Chapter 7
Sink or Swim—
Where is the Capital?

A couple of weeks prior to that stunning announcement of January 26, Skip and CG had arranged for a courtesy call with the leadership of the New York regional office of the FDIC— one of six such offices in the country. They felt it was high time to get to know some of the FDIC people, since it was the bank's secondary regulator and neither of them had previously worked closely with that organization.

So, one day in early February, Skip and CG caught an early train to the Big Apple— prepared just to introduce themselves and share their preliminary plans to resuscitate the embattled thrift.

"We're thinking all we're doing is going up to make this courtesy call," Skip remembers. "We were there in what we thought would be a relaxed format to say, 'Here's what we're doing. We've got this plan. We just finished adequately identifying the problem assets and this is what we are doing about it.'"

After waiting several minutes, the duo were ushered into a large conference room, where New York Regional FDIC Director Nick Ketcha sat surrounded by several of his assistants. But neither Skip nor CG were even given the chance to break the ice.

"Nick Ketcha would have none of it. He didn't even say 'hi' to us. The first words out of his mouth were, '37 million dollar loss, where's the capital?' Skip recalls. "I mean, if he said that once he probably said it at least a dozen times. The meeting lasted 20 minutes at most. In essence he said, 'Unless you raise capital, you're history. Tell us what you're going to do about raising capital— right now. Where's the capital?' That's all he said. He would not engage in any conversation whatsoever."

While it was certainly not the anticipated warm introductory meeting, Skip concedes that Mr. Ketcha's intensity was not at all unreasonable.

"He had every right to ask that question. We had less than $5 million in capital supporting about $1.5 billion in assets. WSFS was about $70 million short of the required capital level, and as of year-end 1990, WSFS' core capital ratio was .28% compared to a required 4%. So his question and focus on it were absolutely appropriate with the value of hindsight, but it caught CG and me completely off-guard. We had been expecting a friendly get-acquainted meeting where we talked about our preliminary plans, but we never even got to say hello."

From the FDIC's side of the table, Mr. Ketcha's approach to WSFS was exactly in line with the strategy that the organization had adopted toward struggling banks at the time. Simply put, the FDIC couldn't afford to take any obvious risks— billions of dollars were already imperiled by the dozens of thrifts across the country that wouldn't survive the crisis. So, the agency was championing a "show me" attitude.

"My thought at the time was, 'Hey, I know what you can do as a good manager, but there are some things even a good manager can't do,'" Mr. Ketcha recalls. "That was the recollection I had when I started meeting with Skip. We laid that out pretty good. We said, 'The monkey is on your back. We'll give you some room but you have to show us you are capable of executing what you say.'"

The first step of "showing us" would be the capital plan. We are going to take a pause in the story of this disastrous FDIC visit to talk about it here.

Whenever a bank did not meet mandatory capital levels, it was required to create a plan that outlined the actions it would take to come into capital compliance, within a reasonable period of time. Naturally, the severity of the shortfall from required capital levels would dictate how ambitious the plan had to be.

How does a bank not in capital compliance get back there? There are essentially five ways:

- Increase earnings by cutting expenses.
- Retain all earnings (i.e. not paying any dividends to stock-holders).
- Reduce the size of the company so less capital is required.
- Sell assets that have market values greater than their book value.
- Raise new capital by selling newly issued stock.

The more ambitious the plan, of course, the greater the doubt that all actions could be accomplished— so it was the responsibility of regulators to evaluate its soundness and likelihood of success. An approved plan would become a contract between the bank and the primary regulator: in this case, the OTS. But until that authorization went through, the financial institution would be operating under a condition in which the regulator could choose to close it at any time.

WSFS had fallen out of capital compliance by the end of the second quarter of 1990. As a result, the previous management team had begun work on a capital plan in the second half of the year. But as the need for additional writedowns intensified during that period— and the rift of capital shortfall kept widening exponentially— that preliminary plan had to be constantly revised. Until the final size of that rift was known, there was no chance the OTS would approve any plan.

CG inherited this urgent situation when he became chairman in August of 1990, passing it on to Skip when he started in November. Needless to say, the $37 million loss in the fourth quarter that captured Mr. Ketcha's attention had really complicated the problem. At this point, the circumstances at WSFS had become so dire that the bank's capital plan had to be airtight. Otherwise, it simply had no future.

Out of necessity, some of the five aforementioned initiatives were in the planning stages before CG became chair; some had already begun. But the implementation really started in earnest in the first and second quarters of 1991, long before the capital plan would be approved in its final form. The key components were:

1. Significant reduction in expenses, including layoffs.
2. Sale of mortgage servicing rights.
3. Sale of various securities from the investment portfolio.
4. Sale of the automobile fleet leasing subsidiary.
5. Sale of the credit card portfolio.
6. Recapture of overfunding in the pension plan.
7. Sale of offices in Kent and Sussex counties.
8. Raising new capital through the sale of convertible preferred stock.

The first six of these were relatively easy to accomplish, and were all done or well on their way to being done by the summer of 1991. Cumulatively, they were very important, but it was the last two that were absolutely essential to WSFS' future success. The hitch: Those last two measures would also be the most difficult to achieve. Furthermore, raising new capital had a unique twist to it, which we will discuss in the next chapter.

For now, we turn back to CG and Skip walking out of the New York FDIC office in January of 1991.

The Napkin Plan

As told above, Mr. Ketcha recalled telling Skip and CG that the FDIC was going to give WSFS some room, provided they were "capable of executing" what they'd promised.

But Skip and CG didn't hear anything resembling that idea. Reeling from the meeting, the two looked for a good spot to collect their thoughts before heading back to Delaware. "We got back to Penn Station much earlier than we had planned. We sat at one of the aluminum-top tables that were sprinkled in front of the various food court vendors, and literally began to talk about what we are going to do differently than we were planning," Skip recalls.

As discussed above, the bank already had a fairly complete capital plan. The plan did contemplate raising capital, but not until late 1992— which, based on what they just heard, would be far too late for Mr. Ketcha with his insistence that the capital raising should have happened yesterday, if not sooner. The trouble was, WSFS was in such bad shape that Skip and CG knew it was impossible to move that date forward. In addition, until the capital plan was approved, no investor would commit to investing anything: They would be crazy to put money forward without the assurance that the bank wouldn't be closed at the drop of the regulators' hat.

"That realization put us almost in a panic mode," Skip remembers. Rather than resort to hysteria, though, the two men took a pragmatic approach. To save the bank, they knew that they would at least have to show progress on their initial measures towards rescuing it. The only problem: they didn't have a notebook on hand to jot down some ideas.

"So we sat in Penn Station with a napkin and started to lay out how we might begin to raise capital in the near term when we didn't think we had any realistic chance of being successful. We realized that at a minimum, we had to make an effort, sooner than anticipated."

Although the original napkin has long since disappeared, the ideas that were scrawled on it— like how to find investors that would consider agreeing to work with WSFS, even though the bank was in a desperate situation— were crucial to the path the leadership would take.

"The main thing was, we have to start taking concrete action so we can demonstrate to the regulators that we're serious about raising capital," Skip remembers.

The first step coming out of the napkin plan was the decision to hire a regional investment banking firm, Alex Brown & Company, and specifically a man named Don Delson, who years later would become a director of WSFS. His job would be to help the bank put together an investor's book that presented WSFS' situation at a high level, with enough specificity so that potential investors could make a decision about potentially investing once the capital plan was approved.

While the capital plan had envisioned such a book later down the road, the napkin plan changed that timeline to ASAP. Due to that acceleration, Skip and CG were able to send out the investor's book by late in the first quarter of 1991; by the time of that June 19 board meeting discussed in the Introduction, several individuals had signed non-binding letters of intent to make substantial investments in WSFS. Although nothing was set in stone, at least there were people out there who had enough confidence in CG and Skip to make a preliminary commitment. That evidence was part of convincing the regulators to let Skip and the team 'keep the keys.'

The 'Liquidation' Exam

While WSFS worked diligently to gain a firm grasp of its challenges and begin addressing them, loan by loan, the regulatory climate was heating up. The OTS regular exam had been delayed from November 1990, but it was now scheduled to begin in February— shortly after the New York FDIC visit. However, it would not be just the OTS involved, as originally anticipated: As Mr. Ketcha so clearly communicated, the 1990 year-end losses had attracted the FDIC to the party in a major way, with an unexpected mission.

The OTS would follow "normal" examination protocols— to the extent that "normal" could apply to an institution in as bad a shape as WSFS. The exam would chiefly be concentrating on asset valuations and loan loss reserve adequacy, while also scrutinizing the quality and feasibility of the capital plan. Leading this effort in the field would be an Examiner in Charge ('EIC')— usually a senior middle manager working their way up the regulatory organization ladder of success. But in an interesting and providential twist to the WSFS saga, the EIC appointed was Robert P. Gough, a more experienced regulator who was in the twilight of his career. At one point, he had even served as a regional FDIC director (while in a different region, the same position as Nick Ketcha), meaning that he'd spent many years viewing banks from a high level. This was significant.

"Unlike someone building their career, who would likely be very cautious, Bob had a much different perspective," Skip recalls. "Bob and I developed a really great rapport. I respected him, and he seemed to sincerely respect me, and recognizing that what I was doing was in fact the right things for the bank. On more than one occasion, he would say to me, 'You are doing everything to save this bank that the FDIC would do if they took it over.'"

Critically, Skip and Mr. Gough had the same objective: they wanted to save WSFS. While he was still the regulator— the constructive pessimist in the room, by trade— Mr. Gough genuinely seemed to want the best for the Wilmington thrift. And because of his background, he had clout and respect within both federal organizations.

"I think that's part of the story of how we were able to get through the crisis: It took a healthy amount of regulatory courage, and Bob was a big part of that," Skip recalls.[20]

The exam proceeded with the usual ups and downs. Sometime in the second quarter, Mr. Gough was finally able to share some good news: As a result of the bank's very large charge-off in the fourth quarter (and the reason for all of those sensational, doomsday stories in the papers as well as the undivided attention of Mr. Ketcha and the FDIC), the bank was over-reserved. In other words, the WSFS team had projected a greater loss than what the OTS was anticipating, to the tune of $10 million to $15 million. That conclusion was crucial to the bank's eventual success, and shows the wisdom of the very conservative analysis that Skip had directed PwC to undertake in late 1990.

As the meeting with Mr. Ketcha had demonstrated, however, the very large losses had attracted lots of negative attention from the FDIC, propelling them to join the OTS exam in force. They set in motion a separate process that would run in a parallel timeline, for the following reason: If WSFS did end up being closed, (which from a regulatory point of view seemed highly likely), then it would be the job of the FDIC to determine what parts of the bank could be sold to other financial institutions and at what price.

---

[20] See further discussion of Regulatory Courage in Skip's Reflections at the end of this book.

"I do not know the official name of that exam, but once I learned about it, I called it the 'liquidation exam.' It scared the heck out of me," Skip remembers. "Wilmington is a relatively small city in a small state. Even though the FDIC was very discrete, I did not think there was any chance this could be kept secret. Once it became known, it would have become a self-fulfilling prophecy. If a $37 million loss stimulated a mini run on the bank, imagine the reaction to a headline something like, 'FDIC Planning to Close WSFS!' I felt that once that train left the station, that is, the liquidation exam began, WSFS was history."

This was the other side of the gambit in the instructions to PwC to "be conservative." It almost backfired. How could Skip possibly stop that locomotive from pulling away?

He had to take immediate action: Once the press ran with such a story, there would likely be a catastrophic run on the bank, and those hard-won investors would certainly bail out. WSFS would crumble.

"As a result, I made numerous requests to Nick Ketcha and his assistant regional director Michael Perachi to not start the exam," Skip recalls. "They steadfastly refused to even discuss it."

In fact, the *News Journal* reporter covering WSFS did learn of that special exam, and was faced with a decision that could have changed the bank's future. These details are explained in the story on page 125. But Skip could only focus on the factors under his control.

If You Don't Ask, You Don't Get

What do you do when you think your death warrant is about to be issued and the sheriff won't even talk about it? Skip remembers that one morning he was walking around the bank, talking to various Associates, when a particularly bold idea popped into his head.

"I decided to call Dick Stone, who was Nick Ketcha's boss in Washington, D.C.," Skip said. To call it an audacious move would be an understatement: Regional FDIC directors like Mr. Ketcha were revered as god-like in their domains. The FDIC was a non-political organization, and jumping the chain of command— going above the head of a regional director—was looking for trouble.

"You didn't mess around with regional directors because they could put you out of business in a heartbeat," Skip explained. "While I don't remember my exact thoughts, it was probably something like, 'you have nothing to lose.'"

Incredibly, after a few rings, Mr. Stone picked up Skip's call himself— giving WSFS Skip a fighting chance to express the reason for appeal.

"In the span of probably about 20 minutes, I presented my thoughts to Mr. Stone," Skip recalls. "And then, in what can only be called a stunning development, he agreed to let me come to Washington to make my case about WSFS. He did this without talking to Mr. Ketcha."

The meeting was set up for two or three weeks later, and the call was over.

Amazed, Skip felt like he had to try to protect himself from the anticipated wrath of Mr. Ketcha when he found out that Skip had bypassed him. So, he took the initiative— he dialed Mr. Perachi, the assistant regional director, to "confess his sin."

"He said 'You did what?' And then there was silence at the other end of the phone for 20 or 30 seconds. He asked that question two more times while I remained silent and then said, 'I've got to go tell Mr. Ketcha.' He just hung up without a word."

Feeling like he'd just tipped a bottle of gasoline over a smoldering fire, Skip braced himself for the likely consequences of his actions: the cancellation of the D.C. meeting with Mr. Stone. Going over the head of a superior in such a big bureaucratic organization was corporate suicide, and Skip knew that. So, when the meeting was not called off, he was quite surprised. It was time to prepare.

Saved by... a Bedsheet?

In March 1991, Skip boarded a Washington-bound train for his last chance to beg regulators to put the brakes on the liquidation exam. Though it was a solo mission this time, Skip brought two important things along for the ride: A portable carousel projector— the likes of which few reading this book will probably remember— and a tray of slides. The era of Powerpoint presentations was still years away.

When Skip arrived at the FDIC building, he was led to a conference room by one of Mr. Stone's assistants. Glancing around the walls, he realized that there was a problem: The conference room had no projection screen! He wouldn't be able to show his precious slides; a visual play-by-play of how WSFS planned to battle back from the brink. He turned to the assistant. "Can we get a projection screen?"

"She said, 'I'll have to go look for one,'" Skip remembers. That wasn't a very good sign. After what seemed like an eternity, the woman returned, carrying something white. But it was not a projection screen. It was a bedsheet.

"And this dear lady takes the bedsheet, climbs up on a credenza, and tacks this sheet to the wall so that I can show my slides," Skip remembers with a laugh.

Much to everyone's amusement, Skip was able to go through his entire presentation— probably one of the most important slideshows of his career—with only the occasional wrinkle. Besides being memorable for the tools involved, Skip was able to get his point across in a way that would have been impossible if he'd just made a speech.

"I still remember the sheet," said John Downey in an interview. "But it was so effective because I think if you did it verbally without that type of stuff, you would not get the results that you wanted to get."

Despite the success of the presentation, Skip never got any direct feedback from the meeting. Only at some point later did he learn that the liquidation exam had continued, although quietly. So, while he ultimately wasn't able to stop that exam train from leaving the station, Skip believes that the opportunity the meeting gave him— to express the soundness of WSFS' plans for the future, to share the success the bank already had in implementing some of their strategies, and to discuss the emerging conclusions of the OTS exam— all helped slow the train down, giving WSFS more time. That extra time would prove crucial.

Meanwhile, the 'regular' OTS exam, as previously mentioned, was starting to come up with some definitive information about WSFS' status. In addition to the conclusion that the bank was "over reserved," the field examination team under Mr. Gough's leadership judged the capital plan to be a reasonable strategy to get the bank back on track. However, the two most vital and problematic on that list selling the downstate offices and raising new capital— were yet to be achieved.

The fieldwork portion of the exam was completed in late April. While a draft of the anticipated written exam existed at that point, it would have to go into an extensive review process within the agency— especially given the troubled situation at WSFS— before the exam was finished. This process is basically the same nowadays: Once the agency review is finalized, the field team returns to the bank to meet with the full board, accompanied by one or two more senior regulators.

Deja Vu: "The Keys, Please"

Now, it's time to rewind to the introduction of this book, which retells the highlights of that eventful board meeting on June 19, 1991. A few weeks prior, Mr. Gough had told Skip that about four additional regulators would be joining the bank's usual players in the boardroom that day— more than the typical representation, at one of those field exam conferences, but nothing to be concerned about.

But on that chilly late spring morning where our story began, 13 regulators filed into the boardroom. There was no way they'd been dispatched to communicate anything good.

Sure enough, things quickly unraveled as the morning went on. Instead of granting capital plan approval, as WSFS had been expecting, the regulators painted a dim picture of the bank's future and asked for permission to sell WSFS. The board— most of all Skip— was stunned: A few days prior to the meeting, Mr. Gough had told him to expect smooth sailing. So, needless to say, it was a real shock when the proceedings turned ugly from the opening bell. To this day, Skip doesn't know why the atmosphere in that room was so different from what Mr. Gough had anticipated.

As discussed at the beginning of this book, we know that Skip fought back with an impassioned plea and won WSFS time to again make direct appeals to FDIC and OTS leadership in Washington, D.C.

Or, as CG remembers it: "Skip pushed that tidal wave out the door."

Still, there were bigger hurdles to clear. Would this second trip to Washington be enough to finally convince the regulators that WSFS was as stubborn as a weed, determined to survive?

To the Nation's Capital...Again

The WSFS team could have had the best ideas in the world to save the bank, but without weeks and months to implement some of them, those promises would fall on deaf ears. That's why Skip's second D.C. trip was so crucial: Besides providing another chance for him to make his case to regulators, it would give WSFS more time to prove itself.

As outlined earlier, the capital plan had about eight key initiatives, all but two of which had already been implemented or were nearly complete by the June meeting. Those last two proposals were the most crucial, but also the least likely to be successful.

In Skip's eyes, the goal of selling the company's eight southern branches in Sussex and Dover counties presented a special challenge: In mid-1991, there was not much demand by other banks to acquire excess branches. The OTS was rightly skeptical that WSFS would be able to make good on that idea— and at a profit, to boot. Still, if they were able to pull off the sale, it would be a critical win: shrinking the bank's size and dramatically improving the capital ratio.

As luck would have it, the second trip to Washington provided WSFS a chance to complete the negotiations with Wilmington Trust, which ultimately agreed to purchase the southern branches. Shortly after that, Skip's encore Washington meeting was officially scheduled with Mr. Stone and Mr. Downey. It was starting to seem like fate was rooting for the WSFS squad.

"While the sale had not closed by that point, it was wonderful momentum to be able to go into that meeting with an agreement to accomplish something that most people thought we could not do," Skip recalls.

Feeling energized by that triumph, Skip arrived at the OTS headquarters in D.C., ready to go to bat for WSFS in front of the regulator's key players. But when he was finally led into the conference room, just after lunch, he saw that Mr. Stone was nowhere to be found. Mr. Downey was there with some other OTS personnel, but they were accompanied by only a single representative from the FDIC that Mr. Stone had sent in his place. Surprised and discouraged, Skip mustered the energy to proceed enthusiastically with the presentation, aware that WSFS' survival hung in the balance.

But not everyone was paying attention. As Skip was speaking, the representative from the FDIC was taking an afternoon snooze, periodically jerking up before dozing off again. This did not bode well.

"Here I am arguing for the life of the company, and to a lesser extent, my career, and one of the key people in the room is falling asleep. I wasn't panicked, but talk about high anxiety," Skip remembers. How would the regulators grant WSFS the ability to stay open if one of them had dreamed his way through the finer points of Skip's address?

When the meeting concluded, Mr. Downey and his drowsy companion thanked Skip for coming, and sent him home without an indication of what the next steps would be. He would later learn that because of the announcement of the branch sale, as well as other progress the bank had made on fulfilling central elements of the capital plan proposal, the regulators had already decided to let WSFS move forward.

On September 30, 1991, the capital plan was officially approved—giving WSFS a legal contract to stay in business as long as it adhered to the goals set forth. The nail-biting days, when the bank could have been arbitrarily shut down by anybody who decided that Skip and the team couldn't hack it, were over. Terra Firma, while not yet reached, was at least visible on the horizon. But one more very significant step remained before the phoenix could begin its rise from the ashes in earnest.

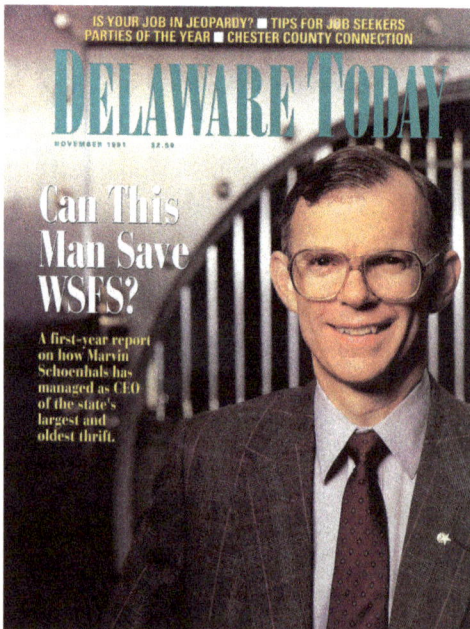

Sidebar: The Reporter Who Could have Closed WSFS

While the regulators descending on WSFS were a nightmare for Skip and his team, one man stood to benefit greatly from the chaotic situation.

In 1991, Peter Osborne was a banking reporter and columnist at the Wilmington *News Journal*. Though he considered himself largely in favor of the financial institutions and other businesses that he covered, much of his work was driven by the use of FDIC and other agency filings to weed out fraud and see the actual numbers behind the press releases.

Cranking out almost a dozen articles a week meant that Peter had sources in high places— including at WSFS, where he had a few connections that even Skip wasn't aware of. So, when Peter received a call the morning of the meeting with regulators tipping him off that there was something going on at the troubled bank, he hurried over to investigate.

"I happened to be downtown," Peter remembers. "This was just before the bank would have opened for the day. I tried to come in, it was early in the morning, and they tried to call up to Skip's office and was told 'he is not available for today.' But there was something going on downstairs that seemed a bit strange, as I recall."

Osborne had been reporting for months about the financial challenges at WSFS and had heard rumblings from employees about the uncertainties around the bank's future, but this was more than that.

"So I called Skip, and he picked up. Because of our relationship, I was direct and said 'I understand there are some regulators in the office...'

"There was dead silence at the other end of the phone. And it wasn't a short dead silence to take a breath. It was a 'clearly you have not anticipated this and you don't have talking points in front of you' type of silence."

Skip's lack of response certainly meant that Peter was on to something. "I had covered these stories when I was in Texas and I knew that you needed to lock down the details before you printed something that would cause a run on the bank, many people to lose their jobs, and a loss of trust in the banking system."

Before calling his editor with the news that WSFS appeared to be on the brink— undoubtedly leading to a front page article with an onerous headline and recognition for being the first to break the story— he took a deep breath and let Skip be the next to speak.

"Skip said something to the effect of, 'this will close us if you print this.' I knew that he had faced this same situation a few times over the previous year or so when we had reported on the write-offs and other problems. He was a good guy who genuinely cared about the people who worked there and about his customers. And you're sitting there thinking, is this really something I want to do?"

After talking to his editor, Peter decided to hold off printing the story. He knew well the value of a good scoop, but was also sensitive about the power his stories could have: Similar news reports were sparking runs on banks across the country at the same time, and that kind of event could ruin WSFS. Instead, he made a deal with Skip that he'd be the first to get any news—good or bad. That access helped him keep his readers informed while giving the WSFS team time to work through the issues in a fast-developing situation.

It was a choice that he didn't make lightly, but one he feels right about every time he drives by a WSFS branch near his home in Pennsylvania. If he'd run to press on that fateful spring day of 1991, the bank would have likely been history.

Chapter 8
The Phoenix Rises—
Capital Compliance!

The Investor Chronicles

With the approval of the Capital Plan, WSFS had the crucial green light to begin to rise from the ashes of uncertainty. However, some other green stuff was still missing from the equation, preventing the bank from being able to declare itself officially out of the woods. That, of course, was cold, hard cash— better known as equity capital.

The seemingly most obvious solution to this problem would be to begin raising the required funds to bring the bank into full capital compliance: approximately $40 million. But there was a hitch. While somebody or a group of somebodies might have been willing to write that check, doing so would have cost the bank about $20 million. That's right: Bringing the bank into full capital compliance in one step would have cost the bank a pile of money.

Why? The reason behind that head-scratcher lay in regulations concerning the treatment of tax loss carry-forwards. Over the previous two years, WSFS had accumulated losses of approximately $100 million, but those losses had never been deducted for tax purposes because there had not been sufficient income. In such cases, U.S. tax law allows those losses to be 'carried forward' to future years as deductions, thus reducing taxes in future years. What that meant in the short term for WSFS, then, was that approximately $40 million of future earnings would not be subject to taxes.

But there was a problem hidden in the section of the tax code entitled "Change in Control." If the new money came from new shareholders who ended up owning more than 50% of the company, the IRS would deem that a change in control had taken place. As a result, the tax loss carry-forwards would become so limited as to be virtually worthless. In other words, the company would lose $40 million in future earnings. Since it was quite clear that most of the new money would have to come from new shareholders, this was certainly a conundrum.

With all this in mind, the Capital Plan analysis had shown that the maximum amount of funds that WSFS could raise without eliminating the carry forward was $15 million. The predicament, however, was that $15 million would not bring the bank into full capital compliance. Therefore, the bank would only achieve capital compliance by counting on projected earnings for the next two years. Luckily, that was a short enough period that the regulators were willing to accept it as part of the plan— as long as WSFS could raise a minimum of $10 million in the interim. Any less than that would have required more than two years of projected earnings, which the regulators probably would not have been willing to accept as reasonable.

The next question was how to structure the capital raising effort.

"We reasoned that then-current shareholders should have the first opportunity to invest, but we doubted that we could raise the required $10 million minimum from them alone," Skip recalls. "We were certain we had to have new investors. We deemed it essential, however, that before we ever went public with the capital raising effort, we had to know that we would succeed. We could not afford to announce a capital raising effort and then fail to reach the minimum. Such a failure would have been doomsday— no more WSFS.

"To solve this dilemma, we decided to approach investors with the expertise and capacity to invest in a problem bank like WSFS. We asked them to become 'standby investors' to the rights offering to shareholders. For this to work, standby commitments of $10 million were required. We also determined that the most efficient method for achieving this would be to find a lead investor— someone willing to pledge about $5 million. This kind of commitment could only come from an investor who understood the situation well, thus giving confidence to others to become part of the plan. Our initial efforts were pretty much solely directed toward finding that lead investor, which could finally begin in earnest with the approval of the Capital Plan."

Over the fourth quarter of 1991 and the first quarter of 1992, Skip and the WSFS team began working hard with Alex Brown & Co. to identify potential investors— most importantly, the lead investor. That effort resulted in Alex Brown introducing WSFS to Betsy Cohen, then the head of Jefferson Bank in Philadelphia. While a successful CEO, she was also a well-known investor in the banking sector. Along with her husband, Ed Cohen, a successful investor in the energy industry, she indicated a serious interest in backing the Wilmington thrift as its lead financier.

The Cohens saw two different kinds of opportunities in WSFS. Believing that the bank was a good franchise and if savable if the required capital was raised, an investment in it had the potential to yield tremendous returns. Beyond that, a heavy involvement with the venerable local thrift would extend their banking footprint from Philly into the Delaware market— a move that, with the unique authorities in WSFS's charter, could provide unique national possibilities as well.

After reaching a preliminary agreement with the bank, Betsy hired an outside firm to perform due diligence on the WSFS loan portfolio. They were to repeat the work that had been done by Price Waterhouse in Q4 of 1990 and the OTS in early 1991.

Sometime in late spring of 1992, Skip got a call inviting him to breakfast with Betsy and her husband at the Rittenhouse Hotel, on the famous Rittenhouse Square in downtown Philadelphia. While he had not been told what the meeting would be about, he wasn't concerned as he drove up to Philly that morning. In his mind, the deal had been pretty much finalized. He was very confident in the PwC work.

In a shocking turn of events, the Cohens announced over their eggs and toast that they weren't going to go through with the preliminary deal, or any deal for that matter. They were done with WSFS: Their due diligence team, in contrast to the regulator's decision, had concluded that the bank had not reserved enough for the problem assets..

"Here we went from 'we're on a glidepath to save the bank,' to 'whoa, the glidepath ran into a mountain,'" Skip recalls. Suddenly, he'd lost his appetite. It was yet another disappointment in the bank's tumultuous saga, and one that threatened to squash the team's progress. The light at the end of the tunnel had turned out to be another oncoming train.

When Some Much-Needed Green Came Out of the Blue

Not long after that letdown, Skip got a call from a stranger named Mark Schoeppner. Mark operated his own investment management company— Quaker Capital Management— in Pittsburgh, and kept an eye on local savings and loans. WSFS wasn't much of a stranger to him: His wife had grown up in Wilmington and her parents still lived there, meaning that local WSFS branches were a familiar sight. So, when he came across a WSFS press release one day indicating that the bank was in the process of raising capital, he wanted to learn more.

A short time later, Mark came to Wilmington to meet with Skip. The two spent time discussing the bank and examining documents. Eventually, Mark told Skip that he thought the bank was a worthwhile investment, but his firm wasn't big enough to commit the $5 million that WSFS would be looking for from a lead investor. Nonetheless, he had friends with bigger pocketbooks: He wanted to introduce the WSFS folks to a firm called Quad-C. The key players of Charlottesville, Virginia-based Quad-C were Terry Daniels and Ted Weschler, the latter of whom was a good friend of Mark's from their Wharton days. With the financial size and scope to promise that kind of money, Quad-C could be the answer to WSFS' prayers— if they'd be interested, that is.

Mark walked Ted through the bank's trials and tribulations, and explained how Skip and his team were trying to put together a rights offering.

"Mark and I had talked a lot about the banking sector," Ted recalls. "I knew very little about it analytically, other than I had been a bank teller for three years in college and really loved the workings of the banking system, but I never held myself out as an investor in banks. He was at my house in Virginia and he said, 'I'm looking at this interesting thing up in Delaware. It's too big for me but I think it may be something that you may want to look at.'"

Intrigued, Ted wasted no time in consulting his partner Terry Daniels. "I said, 'Here's the situation,'" Ted recalls. "'This institution, founded in 1832, clearly has difficulties. My friend Mark, who I've got a lot of respect for, thinks highly of this management team, thinks it's a reasonable deal, and thinks that it's something that could make sense.' My partner was like, 'Wow, that actually sounds like there's a franchise there. Yeah, let's dig into it.'"

This time, Ted and Terry both came to Wilmington to meet with Skip in his office at 838 Market Street. The trio hit it off: Ted and Terry quickly realized that Skip was a straight-shooter, with significant regulatory credibility from his work in Michigan, and Skip concluded that the other two guys were astute investors.

A few weeks later, Ted again journeyed to Wilmington along with Mark. This trip was chiefly for the purpose of research: They spent most of their time going over a spreadsheet that Mark had built of the WSFS loans. As they studied the situation on paper, they became convinced that the bank could not only survive, but prosper.

That verdict led to another field trip for Skip to meet with Ted and Terry on their home turf.

Sweating it Out in Charlottesville

Terry's name was recognizable for a reason: He was known in financial circles as an experienced leader and investor. When he and Ted first met, Terry had been vice-chairman of the WR Grace company. When he eventually left WR Grace, Ted followed a few months later, and the two men hatched the idea to start Quad-C: A hedge fund investing in unique situations in both public and private companies. In other words, Terry was familiar with the kinds of circumstances WSFS found itself in. So, when he and Ted invited Skip and the PwC accountant in charge of WSFS' affairs to meet with him at his home in Charlottesville, there was no saying no.

It was late morning by the time Skip and Vicky Wilson—the partner from PwC in charge of the WSFS relationship—arrived at Terry's sprawling residence at the base of the Blue Ridge Mountains. The high sun made for a beautiful day, to be sure, but it also made for one pretty uncomfortable WSFS CEO: Skip was already sweating in his pressed suit and tie, and the meeting hadn't even begun.

As it turned out, he would soon have a partner in perspiration: Terry had apparently just finished weed whacking in the heat, and was visibly sweat-soaked as he came over to meet his guests. He looked more like a farmer coming in from the field than a hedge fund expert on the cusp of discussing the future of WSFS, but at least it meant he was laid back. The group of four exchanged pleasantries and sat down to chat—unfortunately, still in direct sunlight.

From there, things began to roll along as planned, until Terry turned to Vicky with a simple question. "Is the loan loss reserve accurate?"

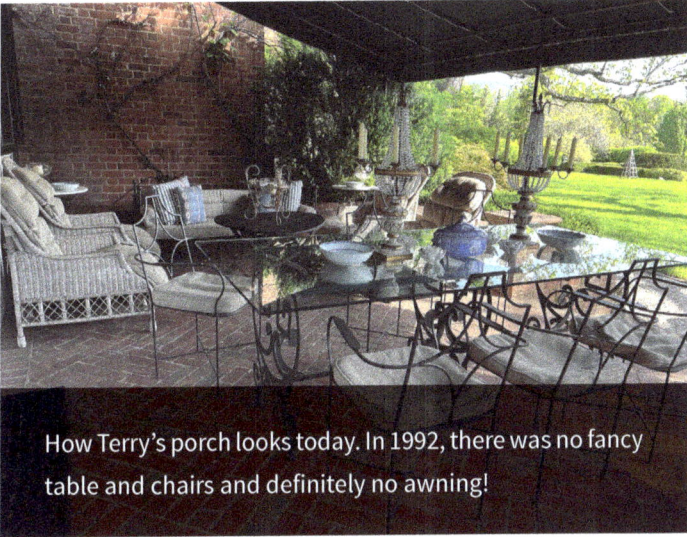

How Terry's porch looks today. In 1992, there was no fancy table and chairs and definitely no awning!

"That was kind of Terry's style to go straight for the jugular on something like that," Ted recalls of his partner's no-holds-barred approach. "He asked that as kind of the final question, to get affirmation and put pressure on Vicky to make sure that it continued to be the truth going forward."

Most public accountants would be quite cautious in answering such a question, and give a highly qualified answer. Maybe it is, maybe it isn't, and here's why— like lawyers, they tend to try to avoid strict 'yes' or 'no' responses. But to Skip's astonishment, Vicky answered that query with an emphatic 'yes.'

"To this day, I'm amazed that a partner of a major public accounting firm was willing to make that emphatic statement about how strong the reserves were," Skip recalls. "I was shocked at the certainty of her answer."

"It wasn't necessarily bullet proof. But that said, Terry was the guy who needed to hear it, and he heard it loud and clear. And that gave him a great deal of comfort," Ted remembers.

While Skip may never know exactly what Vicky was thinking as a brand-new partner at PwC, her clear, confident answer had huge ripple effects: It gave Terry and Quad-C the faith to formally proceed with their investment in WSFS.

Not long after that, they agreed to become the bank's lead investor for the rights offering, committing $5 million to the transaction.

"The more we dug into it, the more interesting it was," Ted remembers about Quad-C's decision to back the bank. "The level of work that CG had put into recruiting Skip, and the level that Skip put into responding to this request for a proposal was stunning. Terry and I were like, 'Wow, these are just really serious folks that are thoughtfully approaching this thing.'"

From Ted's perspective, the fact that WSFS had such firm roots in the region— and so much loyalty from its customers— also made it a worthwhile endeavor.

"You look at the institution and it was, as I recall, it was about a billion dollars in assets. At the time, about 161 years old. Customers who were going to leave, deposits that were going to leave, were long gone. This was very sticky money because you had this very old franchise that was definitely integrated into the community."

While having Quad-C on board was a huge win for the WSFS folks, the hedge fund couldn't singlehandedly carry the bank over the threshold to rights offering— even if it had wanted to. The most it could invest was approximately $5 million, which would give them ownership of about 25% of WSFS. If any investor owns more than 25% of a financial institution, they are required to register as a bank holding company, which subjects them to a laundry list of additional regulatory requirements. For that reason, very few regular equity investors, if any, would willingly place themselves in that category. Quad-C was no exception.

WSFS would therefore need standby commitments from additional investors to reach the $10 million threshold. With a bit of patience, perseverance and positivity, the bank locked in eight more investors over the next month or so. Miraculously, the combined pledges reached a total of $10.4 million, guaranteeing that WSFS would cross the finish line.

The list of those investors and amounts committed are shown below. As with much of this story, for some of them their decision to support WSFS in its hoped-for miraculous rise from the ashes went deeper than an opportunity for a significant financial gain. Anyone familiar with Wilmington's past will recognize that six of those eight names were well-known Wilmingtonians; among them John W. Rollins and Verino Pettinaro. But most surprising of all is the fact that Wilmington Trust Company appears right along with them.

Standby Investors for the WSFS Rights Offering of 1992

Quad-C, Inc	$5,000,000
John W. Rollins	$2,250,000
Verino Pettinaro	$1,200,000
Quaker Capital Management	$750,000
The Hillman Company	$500,000
Wilmington Trust Company	$500,000
Marvin N. Schoenhals	$100,000
Joseph R. Julian	$75,000
Thomas C. Shea	$ 50,000

A Trusty Competitor

At the time of the rights offering, Wilmington Trust was the largest and most influential financial institution in Delaware. WSFS, while much smaller, was a competitor with Wilmington Trust, so that begs the obvious question: Why would a competitor be willing to invest— albeit a relatively small amount of $500,000— in helping WSFS survive? And, what's more, why would they be willing to have their name listed publicly as a standby investor?

"To this day, I believe this is one of the most significant examples of capitalism statesmanship," says Skip.

The CEO of Wilmington Trust was a gentleman by the name of Bernard J. Taylor II, known by his friends as Barney.

"Barney and I had developed a working relationship during our negotiations to sell the southern branches of WSFS to Wilmington Trust," Skip recalls— the critical transaction that reduced the size of WSFS while also generating much-needed capital. But as the two got to know each other, Barney also let Skip in on some of his personal thoughts about the challenges facing local banks. "He shared with me that he thought it would be bad for Delaware to have any significant financial institution fail," Skip remembers. "While agreeing to buy the southern branches was a straightforward strategic decision on the part of Wilmington Trust, the willingness to invest in a competitor and do so publicly is a step far beyond just strategic business importance."

Not only did Wilmington Trust's contribution help WSFS make it to that initial $10 million milestone, it also probably influenced other investors as well— enhancing the public's perception of the bank's ability to succeed and thus encouraging others to participate.

As the years went by, Skip and Barney remained close: both wishing they could learn to not swing so hard at a golf ball. Barney retired in 1992 after 13 years at Wilmington Trust, but continued to serve on its board of directors until May 1998. He passed away in August of 2005 at the age of 79.

Also Notable

Two other standby investors deserve comment as well, if purely because of their inspiring personal histories. Until his death in 2000, John W. Rollins was known far and wide as a very successful entrepreneur. But few people know that he grew up dirt-poor in Georgia, scratching together a few dollars by going door to door to sell bedspreads and other household items. In the aftermath of the Great Depression, he left the family farm in Ringgold and moved to Philadelphia. His storied career took off as a series of enterprising ventures, ultimately ending up with the formation of nine NYSE firms and many other initiatives. He and his equally well-known brother, O. Wayne Rollins, also founded Rollins Inc., one of the country's leading pest-control conglomerates. Other listed companies included Dover Downs, Rollins Truck Leasing, Matlack Systems, the country's largest bulk trucking company, and Rollins Purle, which later became Rollins Environmental.

In 1952, Rollins was elected Lieutenant Governor of Delaware, serving four years. By 1963, he was honored with the Horatio Alger Award for distinguished Americans— named after the author who famously wrote stories about young men who worked their way from rags to riches. He later started a scholarship fund, also under Alger's name, for high school students in Delaware who have faced and overcome significant obstacles in their pursuit of higher education.

In the year before Skip became CEO, John had accumulated a position in WSFS stock equal to 10% of the outstanding stock of the company. His investment was based on a gut feeling: After watching a stock that had originally been issued at about $10 a share that had gone to about $22, and now was selling at less than $2 a share, he figured it was likely a very good investment. On that hunch, he purchased approximately $1 million of stock in WSFS. For the 'Rights Offering,' he agreed to become one of the standby investors, committing an additional $2.25 million, which would bring his ownership interest to 14%.

The other significant local investor was Verino Pettinaro— another man with a story that could have come from the mind of author Horatio Alger. Starting as a humble local contractor doing modest home additions, he eventually became one of the most well-known real estate tycoons in the Delaware Valley.

Similar as they were, neither John nor Verino had spoken with each other about their investments in WSFS. If they had, they would have known that they both, in fact, had accumulated about 10% of the company in the year before Skip's ascension to CEO. That news finally dawned on them when the company published its 1990 annual report. Verino also became a standby investor so that he could maintain his 9.9% ownership interest. As of the date of this book, Verino is still alive, and his company has continued under the leadership of his son.

The Next Steps

With the fulfillment by standby investors of the $10 million minimum, the bank went ahead with the rights offering to shareholders, which raised a total of $13.4 million as of September 1992. That capital would be in the form of a convertible preferred stock— carrying a 10% interest rate and convertible into six shares of common stock. Each preferred share was sold for an initial price of $9 per share, setting the underlying price in terms of common stock at $1.50 per share.

The closing of the preferred stock sale marked a significant leap forward for WSFS in the course the bank had charted toward full regulatory capital compliance. As explained elsewhere, the size of the new capital had to be limited so as to protect the net operating tax loss carry-forward. Nonetheless, acquiring that capital was the single most important step in the plan, which anticipated reaching full capital compliance by the end of 1994 as a result of projected earnings in 1993 and 1994.

In his Letter to Shareholders in the 1992 Annual report, Skip began: *"It is with great pleasure that I am able to report that 1992 was a turnaround year for Star States Corporation. The results of the first full year following the approval of our Capital Plan and completion of our internal restructuring activities exceeded expectations. Additionally, these results were achieved despite continued sluggishness in the regional and national economies.*

Foremost during 1992, Star States was able to complete a $13.4 million placement of convertible preferred stock. Net proceeds of $11.8 million were used to recapitalize the Company's principal subsidiary, Wilmington Savings Fund Society, FSB (WSFS or Bank). Led by our improved operating performance and capital ratio, confidence among our customers and community as a whole has been renewed."

The End of the Tunnel

While the above milestone was indeed cause for celebration, 1993 would offer the bank an extraordinary opportunity that would ultimately fast-track its capital compliance timetable. After years of near despair, financial markets had recovered so strongly from 1990 that there was a great deal of liquidity, as evidenced by an improving economy and bank stock prices in particular. These factors would make it possible for some companies to raise quantities of money that would have seemed like pipe dreams not long before.

Sensing an opportunity afoot, the WSFS leaders decided to take advantage of the favorable market conditions. In the second half of 1993, less than a year after the preferred stock sale, they set out to determine if the bank could issue 'senior notes' at the holding company level.

Senior notes are generally considered higher-quality bonds, but given the financial condition of WSFS at the time, they might have appropriately been called 'junk bonds' (named like that because of their high risk). If issued directly by a bank, they would not normally count as regulatory capital for that bank. However, under a unique quirk in the rules for savings and loan holding companies like WSFS, a holding company could issue debt in the form of senior notes, but then downstream the proceeds to the bank as equity capital.

Complicated though that may sound, the bottom line was this: If WSFS could issue enough of these bonds by the last day of 1993, the bank could achieve capital compliance a year earlier than expected. That fact would then be reflected in year-end databases for 1993— enabling the bank to potentially pursue opportunities to acquire the assets of other financial institutions that had failed.

But they had to act fast; The end of December was quickly approaching. So, on December 29,1993, the bank closed a whopping (relative to its size at the time) $32 million worth of 11% senior notes. Despite that high interest rate, the tremendous value of the downstreamed equity capital was worth it.

A mere two days later, on December 31, the bank finally reached that lofty, long sought-after milestone of full capital compliance. The road had been long and bumpy, full of twists and turns—but the hardy bank had prevailed, along with its tenacious leaders.

"To this day, I am still amazed that we were able to issue what I considered essentially equity, but in the form of debt," Skip remembers. "This had the advantage of achieving full capital compliance, while not impacting the net operating loss carry forward, and at no significant dilution to shareholders."

The structure of the senior notes was such that it encouraged the early conversion of the previously issued convertible preferred stock. In order to facilitate that conversion, which occurred in April of 1994, preferred shareholders were offered 6.47 shares instead of the original 6 shares— thus reducing their conversion price to $1.39 per share from $1.50 per share. As a result, preferred shareholders agreed to the change.

While a bank holding company issuing senior notes was not all that unusual, very few issued senior notes that would be labeled 'junk bonds,' and even fewer could say that those 'junk bonds' played a starring role in helping them achieve such an important benchmark.

With WSFS fully capital compliant, the first chapter of the Skip Schoenhals Saga came to a close. The bank could now concentrate on its plan for the future: To become a vibrant financial institution in the Delaware market. It was free of all regulatory constraints— other than those applied to any financial institution under normal circumstances—and could finally use the creativity of the board, management, and the communities it served to grow into a truly distinguished company.

The exhilaration of that moment was captured in the opening lines of Skip's 1993 Letter to Shareholders:

"It is my distinct pleasure to report a series of extraordinary accomplishments in 1993 by a group of talented and dedicated people on behalf of WSFS Financial Corporation and its principal subsidiary, Wilmington Savings Fund Society, FSB (WSFS).

*Following the completion of a $32 million private placement of 11% Senior Notes, and the subsequent infusion of capital into WSFS, the institution as of December 31, 1993 was in full compliance with the regulatory capital requirements of the Office of Thrift Supervision (OTS). In addition, WSFS has been classified as an 'Adequately Capitalized' financial institution and the OTS Capital Directive was removed, as well as **all outstanding actions against WSFS.***"

The Phoenix had indeed taken flight.

The following page is a reproduction of the first page of the Letter to Shareholders that appeared in the 1993 Annual Report to Shareholders.

MARVIN N. SCHOENHALS, CHAIRMAN, PRESIDENT AND CEO, WSFS FINANCIAL CORPORATION

I T IS MY DISTINCT PLEASURE TO REPORT A SERIES OF EXTRAORDINARY ACCOMPLISHMENTS IN 1993 BY A GROUP OF TALENTED AND DEDICATED PEOPLE ON BEHALF OF WSFS FINANCIAL CORPORATION AND ITS PRINCIPAL SUBSIDIARY, WILMINGTON SAVINGS FUND SOCIETY, FSB (WSFS).

FOLLOWING THE COMPLETION OF A $32 MILLION PRIVATE PLACEMENT OF 11% SENIOR NOTES, AND THE SUBSEQUENT INFUSION OF CAPITAL INTO WSFS, THE INSTITUTION AS OF DECEMBER 31, 1993, WAS IN FULL COMPLIANCE WITH THE REGULATORY CAPITAL REQUIREMENTS OF THE OFFICE OF THRIFT SUPERVISION (OTS). IN ADDITION, WSFS HAS BEEN CLASSIFIED AS AN "ADEQUATELY CAPITALIZED" FINANCIAL INSTITUTION AND THE OTS HAS TERMINATED THE CAPITAL DIRECTIVE AND REMOVED ALL OUTSTANDING ACTIONS AGAINST WSFS.

TANGIBLE, CORE, AND RISK-BASED CAPITAL RATIOS AT DECEMBER 31, 1993, WERE 6.35%, 6.39% AND 9.74%, RESPECTIVELY.

ACHIEVING CAPITAL COMPLIANCE AND THE SUBSEQUENT REMOVAL OF ALL EXTRAORDINARY REGULATORY RESTRICTIONS A FULL YEAR AHEAD OF SCHEDULE, PUT US SIGNIFICANTLY CLOSER TO REALIZING OUR VISION. WE NOW HAVE THE RESOURCES AND THE CAPACITY TO SEIZE NEW OPPORTUNITIES FOR GROWTH, TO EXPAND THE FRANCHISE OF WSFS AND TO ACTIVELY PURSUE BUSINESSES THAT OFFER THE GREATEST RETURN ON INVESTMENT.

A DETAILED STRATEGIC PLAN WITH AMBITIOUS GOALS FOR 1994 AND BEYOND IS IN PLACE. AS YOU READ THE COMMENTS OF THE PEOPLE WHO WILL LEAD OUR FIVE BUSINESS UNITS TOWARD THOSE GOALS, YOU WILL UNDERSTAND MY CONFIDENCE IN OUR ABILITY TO REACH A WIDE RANGE OF SHORT- AND LONG-TERM OBJECTIVES.

THESE MANAGERS HAVE THE ADDED ADVANTAGE OF SUPPORT FROM A STAFF OF HIGHLY COMPETENT AND HARD WORKING ASSOCIATES, WHOSE EFFORTS WERE KEY IN THIS TRANSFORMATION. WITH THEM, WE ARE CONFIDENT OF THE ULTIMATE SUCCESS OF OUR MISSION: TO BECOME A PREMIER COMMUNITY-BASED FINANCIAL INSTITUTION DEDICATED TO MAXIMIZING STOCKHOLDER VALUE, WHILE MAKING THE NAMES WSFS AND FIDELITY FEDERAL SYNONYMOUS WITH VALUE, QUALITY AND SERVICE.

RECAPITALIZATION MARKS THE POINT WHERE WE CAN BEGIN TO MOVE WITH AN EYE TO THE FUTURE. WHAT WAS ACHIEVED IN 1993, HOWEVER, DESERVES SPECIAL REVIEW.

• NET INCOME FOR THE YEAR WAS $6.4 MILLION, UP MORE THAN 30% OVER 1992.

• TOTAL NONPERFORMING ASSETS WERE REDUCED TO $51.1 MILLION AT DECEMBER 31, 1993, DOWN FROM $75.8 MILLION AT DECEMBER 31, 1992. IN THE FOURTH QUARTER ALONE, NONPERFORMING ASSETS WERE REDUCED BY $19.4 MILLION.

• MORTGAGE ORIGINATIONS TOTALED MORE THAN $122 MILLION IN 1993, MAKING WSFS A LEADER IN THE RESIDENTIAL MORTGAGE MARKET IN NORTHERN DELAWARE.

DURING THE PAST YEAR, THE WSFS TEAM OF ASSOCIATES WAS FURTHER ENHANCED BY THE ADDITION OF TWO INDIVIDUALS TO OUR SENIOR STAFF, AS WELL AS TWO NEW MEMBERS TO THE BOARD OF DIRECTORS.

R. WILLIAM ABBOTT, EXECUTIVE VICE PRESIDENT AND CHIEF FINANCIAL OFFICER, BRINGS 30 YEARS OF FINANCIAL INSTITUTION EXPERIENCE TO WSFS. THE BREADTH OF HIS KNOWLEDGE MAKES HIM A PARTICULARLY VALUABLE RESOURCE FOR THE COMPANY.

ALSO, FRANCIS J. PENNELLA JOINED THE COMPANY AS SENIOR VICE PRESIDENT, RETAIL LENDING DIVISION. FRANK'S 25 YEARS OF BROAD-BASED BANKING EXPERIENCE GREATLY

Chapter 9
Sowing the Seeds

On January 2, 1994, the first working day of that year, members of the WSFS management team were finally able to come into the office feeling confident that they had a secure future. It was time, once and for all, to turn their attention to rebuilding the venerable Delaware institution for upcoming generations.

The aim was for WSFS to leverage its legacy as a longstanding source of consumer-oriented home mortgage financing, and to cautiously move in the direction of adding more robust business banking products and services. As detailed earlier, the previous management team had taken steps in that direction, but with disastrous results. To avoid a repeat of their mistakes, the team had to go back to square one and begin that building-out process all over again: Hiring new people, developing new products, and establishing the necessary infrastructure to become a viable business banking institution in the Delaware market. If all went well, the bank's reputation for excellence would be restored, and it would once again be regarded as a valuable investment for shareholders.

Morale was sky-high within the WSFS offices as the bank's leaders developed a strategic plan to sow the seeds of the future. They started by articulating the vision for the company, which stands to this day: To be an independent, community bank, that would create value for shareholders as a result of outstanding customer relationships. This meant meeting the needs of each customer with a personalized approach— getting to know them and earning their trust while helping them achieve their financial goals.

Beyond that focus on a strong, connected client base, the performance side of the bank's activities would be directed toward always "earning the right to remain independent." The first steps toward that mission were to add new products in home equity lending, and to re-enter the credit card business. The changed prospects were immediately evident in the bank's 1994 first quarter report to shareholders, where Skip could report that WSFS had returned to the "Billion Dollar Club." After three years of shrinking— from $1.6 billion to less than a billion at its lowest point— WSFS was finally starting to make up for lost ground.

OUR VIEW

THE WSFS COMEBACK

A steady hand and tough measures save a thrift

WHERE WE STAND
Back from the brink and over a billion.

The story of Wilmington Savings Fund Society's near fall and rise is an unlikely one. WSFS, a trusted local thrift, got caught up in the cheap thrills of deregulation and reached the brink of extinction. Nothing symbolized its problems more than the disintegration of its new corporate entity, Star States. The dream of Star States transformed from the dream of being known for producing the tallest building in Wilmington to being known for producing "the hole in the ground" at 11th and King streets.

The landscape was pretty bleak for WSFS when Marvin N. "Skip" Schoenhals, a "bank doctor" from the Midwest, was brought in to try to stanch the hemorrhage. Local prognosticators gave him about a 1-in-25 chance of pulling it off. The Resolution Trust Corp., the federal agency responsible for cleaning up the savings fund mess, was poised to deliver the *coup de grace*.

Mr. Schoenhals talked Resolution Trust into giving WSFS one last chance. He sold off some prize assets, WSFS's Kent County operations and the B. Gary Scott real estate company among them. He retained others, including four branches in Philadelphia. He got rid of an expensive pension plan and reduced employees. He turned to speculators to pull his capital ratio back into compliance with federal mandates with a large stock issue, much of which went to high-risk investors such as John W. Rollins Sr. That got the bank back in the serious loan business. WSFS was then positioned to take advantage of the low interest rates that Washington induced. WSFS was able to take great advantage of the home refinancing boom.

Through all of this, Mr. Schoenhals, an unpretentious man whose personal life exemplifies the Christian principles he believes in, quietly moved WSFS further and further out of danger. WSFS is still not out of the woods (its stockholders still don't get paid dividends), but it can see the edge of the forest. In the first quarter of 1994, WSFS began to grow for the first time in three years, once again becoming a billion-dollar company.

WSFS — and Delaware — was lucky to get a businessman like Mr. Schoenhals. We wish him continued success.

The News Journal ran this editorial recognizing the milestone that WSFS had achieved.

Despite what was lost during those three years of 'survival mode,' however, it's important to acknowledge what was strengthened: the entrepreneurial spirit that enabled the company to overcome the incredible obstacles it faced. Now, that same spirit had space and fertile soil to put down roots.

The first move of this new era that some would consider 'out of the box' thinking was to establish a new consumer finance subsidiary called Community Credit Company (CCC), opening its initial office in the Penn Mart Shopping Plaza in New Castle, Delaware in 1994. It was an initiative with a noble goal: to originate first and second mortgages to borrowers with some blemishes on their credit history. What started as a sapling would become a mighty oak tree— this market would eventually come to be known as the 'subprime mortgage' market, a huge segment of the consumer lending world.[21]

Sticking with the theme of the metaphorical WSFS garden, there was another notable seed growing that had been planted much earlier. In 1988, the bank made a loan to a New Jersey company called American Homestead (AH), a private company specializing in originating reverse mortgages. No one thought too much of it at the time, but the transaction would cause quite a few headaches for WSFS during the tumultuous years of 1990-1993. In 1994, however, the bank took a very unusual, entrepreneurial step that would become another tall oak tree in the WSFS forest.

Reverse Mortgages, Explained by Skip Schoenhals

While most readers of this book will be very familiar with conventional home mortgage loans, reverse mortgages may sound like some kind of sorcery. So, let's start with a brief explanation:

A reverse mortgage loan is where a lender sends a monthly check to the homeowner. For those of you just learning about this concept, you might be thinking, "Where do I sign up for that?"

Reverse mortgages are generally taken out by people who have substantial equity in their home, are over 60 years of age, and would like to increase their monthly cash flow. Still sounds good, right? Well, here's where it gets just a little complicated (and some would say, morbid): Once a lender appraises the property and determines that there is sufficient equity in the home, the lender then looks at the life expectancy of the homeowner, and then how much the value of the property is projected to increase during their life expectancy. Based on that information, the lender determines how much cash can be sent to the homeowner, usually in the form of a monthly check. If the calculation was correct and if the homeowner lives for as long as projected, there should be sufficient equity for the home to be sold and the loan to be paid off in full. While not for everyone, it was just the right solution for a certain group of people.

I first heard of reverse mortgages in the 1970s. At that time, it was just an idea, put forth by academics. To my knowledge no reverse mortgages were being made at that point, but I was intrigued. So, I started a file just to accumulate information about them, thinking it might be something a bank would like to offer. I never had a chance to follow up and never heard much about reverse mortgages over the years.

Fast-forward to 1990, and our meetings with Pricewaterhouse in the 4th quarter of 1990 to review all of the bank's loans. To my surprise, the subject of reverse mortgages came up in one of those initial reviews with the PwC team. I found out about that 1988 deal where WSFS had loaned $10 million to a reverse mortgage company called American Homestead in New Jersey. As it turned out, WSFS was a participant with the lead lender in Philadelphia— The Philadelphia Savings Fund Society, known as PSFS— which had committed another $20 million to AH.

As discussed above, the reverse mortgage loan amount to any one borrower is based upon the value of the property, life expectancy, and assumptions about the value of properties changing over time. The financial formula that American Homestead was using to determine that commitment was based upon a financial model developed by a professor at the Wharton School of Money and Banking at the University of Pennsylvania in Philadelphia.

While that formula may have appeared sound on paper, the PwC team was not convinced. When I sat down with them to look at the initial loan reviews, they informed me that in their opinion, the financial model was deeply flawed. Their analysis showed that at some point in the future, the contractual advances required for each reverse mortgage would exceed the future values of the underlying properties.

This was a significant discovery, because a reverse mortgage could only be paid back from the proceeds of the sale of the house. Even if that sale resulted in a deficit, no additional claim could be made against the assets of the homeowners or their estate. In addition, under the terms of a reverse mortgage, American Homestead had to continue to send the monthly checks to the homeowner until they either moved out or passed away. If the checks stopped for any reason, the entire balance of the loan would automatically be forgiven.

To sum it up, even if AH knew that the value of the house was not going to be sufficient to pay off the loan, the company had to continue to provide advances on the loan, or it would become worthless. As the lender to AH, then, WSFS was in the same position. It had to continue to make advances so AH could continue funding— otherwise, the entire loan would have to be written off. As a result of discovering the flawed formula, WSFS had to write down the value of its loan to AH: Part of that infamously large charge-off in the 4th quarter of 1990.

The situation turned out to be a real head-scratcher. We went to both the lead bank and the borrower to express our concern, but neither party was willing to consider that our analysis was correct. And since we were a participating lender— as opposed to the lead lender— we had no ability to force negotiations with AH. A significant part of the problem was that PSFS was also facing mounting financial challenges, so its leaders did not seem too interested in an impartial analysis of the situation.

In response to those circumstances, WSFS did take one aggressive action that would become important in 1993: We forced the loan to be split into two separate pools of reverse mortgages, out of apprehension that we would lose all control over our portion of the loan if PSFS did indeed fail.

Well, we weren't far off with that preemptive action. PSFS was taken over by the FDIC in 1993, sparking negotiations between WSFS and the FDIC for the bank to acquire the rest of the AH portfolio. With everything that was going on, we deemed it very important to have complete control of the loan. The FDIC understood (and agreed) with our analysis that the loan would eventually become a severe problem, so they eventually sold us the remaining part of the portfolio at a discount from par of 28%. Had we not separated the loans in 1991, we would have had a much more delicate situation.

While a minor part of the story, that transaction with the FDIC resulted in the first "payoff" of our reverse mortgage journey. We had been very conservative in that fourth quarter 1990 write down when we took something like a 50% discount. But based on the 28% discount negotiated with the FDIC, a market value was established that allowed us to write up the balance of the loan, increasing the bank's capital. Following that, WSFS was able to foreclose on the entire AH loan, meaning that the bank was now in control of a pool of 750 reverse mortgages in New Jersey and Pennsylvania.[22]

As a result of that original conclusion by the PwC team, we hired an actuarial consultant and other financial experts to analyze American Homestead's portfolio. Since so few people understood reverse mortgages and there was no 'reverse mortgage industry' to speak of, we became pioneers: Learning the ins and outs of those loans before anyone else. At the time, we were just trying to find a solution to a short-term problem— we never dreamed that reverse mortgages would become one of the best investments we ever made.

If that original loan in 1988 was the first chapter in our reverse mortgage journey, then the above stories were the second and third chapters. October 1994 was to be the beginning of the fourth chapter, for WSFS at least— based on a series of events that had begun three years earlier, unbeknownst to us, across the country in San Francisco.

In 1991, a public company was formed called Providential Home Income Plan, Inc. It was no small potatoes: Providential raised $30 million in an initial public offering. With that capital, the company began making reverse mortgage loans in southern California— using the same flawed formula that American Homestead was using. While it would be some time before they realized that flaw, they were soon hit with a change in accounting rules concerning the recognition of income from those reverse mortgages. As a result, the once high-flying Providential was forced to book a very large loss. Once those numbers were compounded with its regular losses, the picture looked quite different to the one their Initial Public Offering (IPO) suggested.

The domino effect of Providential's poor performance caused it to be taken over by a Boston based-hedge fund, which eventually realized it had overpaid (i.e. it discovered the formula was flawed). In short order, the hedge fund looked to unload Providential on a new buyer. They approached WSFS because of the successful purchase of the American Homestead loan from the FDIC.

Due to our extensive and unique knowledge of reverse mortgages, we weren't afraid to pursue the situation. We bought the company for $24.4 million in 1994. To our knowledge, no one else was interested. The transaction was so unusual that on the day of closing, Providential had about $22 million of cash from that public offering— meaning that from a cash point of view, WSFS actually paid for the transaction with Providential's own money. On the other side of that coin, however, WSFS would be obligated to fund a couple of hundred million dollars of required future payments on the reverse mortgages.

In the blink of an eye (and the transfer of a large sum of money), WSFS had become the owner of another 1,250 reverse mortgages. Combined with the previous loans, that meant the bank likely had the largest private-sector reverse mortgage portfolio in the country.

This story could go on for hours, and we'll pick it up again in the future. For now, reflect on how unusual this transaction was for WSFS. A bank based in Wilmington, with virtually all of its business in Delaware, jumped 3,000 miles and three time zones to acquire a company in an industry which few people even knew existed. Unsurprisingly, naysayers abounded. Soon after the acquisition was announced, I received a call from an institutional investor in WSFS, who minced no words to convey that the transaction was one of the stupidest things he had ever heard of. He went so far as to say that someone in senior management must have a kid in college in California, and they were looking for a way to write off the costs of visiting them. Quite a vote of confidence.

---

[21] So huge as an industry that it would cause the world-wide financial catastrophe known as the 'Great Recession' in 2008. The cause of the catastrophe was fundamentally flawed government policies which were then abused by many lenders. For WSFS, however, it would produce huge acorns for the company and its shareholders, a story we will detail in a chapter in Book 2.

[22] In the coming years AH would demand arbitration with WSFS not once but twice, claiming that we mishandled the servicing of the mortgages and owed them money under the terms of the foreclosure agreement. They lost both times.

Chapter 10
Frothy— For Sale

WSFS marched boldly ahead into 1995. The year made famous by the O.J. Simpson trial would see the bank continue to build momentum with a series of strong moves. After acquiring deposits from a branch of another bank in Middletown, Delaware, WSFS opened its first branch inside a supermarket. In February, WSFS procured the deposits from another bank in Dover, leading to the opening of a second supermarket branch there. As the months went on, the bank sold the branches of its subsidiary, Fidelity Federal Savings and Loan, in Northeast Philadelphia— netting $12 million from the sale thanks to the aforementioned frothy market. It was one more step towards undoing previous management's mistakes, and allowed the bank to recuperate a good part of what had been written off back in 1990 when those branches had been virtually worthless.

With all of these new ventures taking off— and market conditions booming— WSFS' performance began to soar. In a mere 33 months after the convertible preferred stock was issued, the bank's stock price went from $1.37 to the $6.00 range. A return of nearly 350% in less than three years is nothing short of incredible, especially considering WSFS' grim not-so-distant past. Investors, notably those who had stuck with WSFS since the early days, were feeling relieved. For comparison's sake, during this same period, the SNL Thrift Index had appreciated only about 100%.

If WSFS seemed to be cruising down the highway at a healthy 70 miles per hour, what happened next would bring the bank to a screeching halt.

Blindsided at Breakfast

By mid-1995, the market for bank stocks had returned to much more normal levels, and acquirers were again paying premiums for banks— especially ones that had recently firmed up their capital reserves and turned record operating profits.

This fact was not lost on John Rollins and the folks at Quad-C. Stunned by the bank's quick and meteoric rise in worth, Ted, his partner Terry, and John Rollins had come to the conclusion that they had a responsibility to their investors to seize the opportunity offered by such a spectacular return by 'monetizing' (turning a paper profit into cash). They would do this if WSFS could be sold to another institution— a move that promised to thrust the bank into the throes of uncertainty once again.

On the eve of the bank's July 1995 board meeting, Skip received a call from Ted Weschler inviting him to breakfast the next morning. The two had met for casual meals in the past, so Skip sensed nothing strange in the air. They set a time to convene at a hotel a few blocks away from the bank, on North King Street.

The men ordered their usual favorites and sat down for some pre-meeting small talk. But when Ted shared that Quad-C and John Rollins had met the previous day to discuss their investment in WSFS—and, more specifically, their inclination to sell the bank—Skip suddenly began to lose his appetite.

"I was shocked. I had not anticipated it. I felt let down," Skip remembered of his initial reaction to the way the conversation was headed.

Across the way, Ted was acting as the messenger— sent out to convey the news on behalf of his partners, even though he wasn't enthusiastic about the decision himself.

"It was an odd dynamic because I was somewhat resistant. I was the junior partner there," he says now. "Terry had a lot more to say, but it culminated in a meeting of John Rollins, Terry, myself, and Gene Weaver, John's Chief Financial Officer and representative on the WSFS board. For whatever reason I got picked as the guy who should deliver the message to Skip. Yep. That was tough. Because my heart wasn't in it. Forget about the yes or no of whether you should sell. It was a big business regret and it still is.

"Quad-C was a young firm. John Rollins, I think, felt like he had dodged a bullet a bit when WSFS pulled itself from the ashes and that it was working out. John was thrilled that, in effect, we'd collectively saved the bank, but he also saw an opportunity to take some winnings off the table.

Ted recalls that Terry Daniels was also eager to sell: "There were a lot of mergers going on, and it looked like we had this nice strategic position in Delaware and that there were folks that would be interested in it."

He apologized to Skip for not including him in those conversations with John Rollins and Terry, but he emphasized that there hadn't been time. The decision process moved along so rapidly that there had been no opportunity to consult the bank's CEO. Without much further discussion, Skip and Ted left breakfast and walked the awkward two blocks to the bank for the board meeting.

While inside Skip may have felt much like one of the scrambled eggs he'd just eaten, he knew the importance of maintaining a calm and cool exterior. He turned Ted's news over in his mind, examining the possibilities from all angles. Sure, losing yet another job would be agonizingly difficult, especially with everything he'd put into saving WSFS from certain death. But at the same time, Skip had always put shareholders first and foremost, and he felt that his responsibility was to do what was best for them, especially when 41% of them (the total ownership level of Quad-C and Rollins combined) had already 'voted.'

Was selling the bank the right thing for shareholders after all? Skip didn't think so. The short term was one thing, but in the long run, Skip felt that they'd have much more to gain if the bank remained independent. As CEO, he was starting to be able to see the future of WSFS-— and it looked bright.

After reaching the bank, head still spinning, Skip excused himself from Ted and went into his office to call Linda— a much-needed pause to get his equilibrium. He had always prided himself on being a "crisis management guy," and this was a personal crisis, so to speak: not life-threatening. He relayed to Linda what had just happened.

"I remember being, like Skip, stunned. But there's nothing you can do, if they're going to sell it, they're going to sell it, and that wouldn't be the first time that happened to us. So you just kind of take it in stride," Linda recalls.

After their brief chat, Skip set his focus on the meeting, where he would have the chance to convey exactly why he thought this was the wrong choice for WSFS.

Rocking the Boat

The rest of the board members were shocked when Ted started off by explaining the conclusion that Quad-C and John had come to. The bank had just attained that coveted, precious stability it had sought for so long; why force it back into choppy waters? After Ted and Gene made their case for selling, a lively discussion ensued. Skip steadily presented his thoughts on the situation, underscoring the bank's bright future and its ability to perform even better for shareholders if it was just given a bit more time to mature into itself. His sentiments were echoed by Bill Abbott, the bank's CFO. Nevertheless, by the end of the meeting, the board did vote to "explore strategic options" for WSFS— in other words saying that it would begin to look into a sale. Skip was the only director to vote against that proposal.

Under the usual circumstances, such a decision would not be made public immediately. But WSFS was in a unique position: Quad-C and John Rollins owned 41% of the outstanding stock of the company, and were directly represented at the boardroom table. With 41% of shareholders already in favor of selling, that seemed like a done deal. As a result, Skip concluded that a public statement should be issued immediately so as to alert current and potential shareholders of what was perceived to be a likely event.

"Normally, the decision of the board to explore options would be surrounded by a great deal of uncertainty because board members would only possess a relatively small percentage of the stock, and you can't be certain that a majority of shareholders will go along with it," Skip said. "But with two professional investors owning 41% of the stock, it would be pretty certain that the bank would be sold. We had a responsibility to alert the market."

Therefore, not long after that meeting, the bank issued a press release outlining the company's move to explore strategic alternatives. Although still hoping that the sale would not come to pass, Skip dutifully got to work on the process, hiring back Alex Brown to put together another pitch book to show to potential acquirers.

The board anticipated that a number of institutions would be very interested in WSFS— one of the few remaining independent banks of a significant size in Delaware. But as the marketing efforts moved ahead, they were proved wrong.

Over the coming months, several groups reviewed the books, but they would all ultimately decide for a number of reasons that WSFS was not a fit for them.

One deterrent, according to Skip, was the company's significant position in reverse mortgages: Few people understood how they worked, so potential buyers were spooked by the possibility of negative surprises down the line. When bankers look at an unusual type of loan— or at least something they're unfamiliar with— they generally assume the worst, and discount its value. This created a huge disconnect between the perspectives of potential acquirers, and those of the WSFS team, as to the bank's true worth. While the purchasers felt that the reverse mortgages added nothing to the bank's value, Skip, Ted and the others believed them to be even more valuable than what was listed on the balance sheet. Although they turned out to be bad for the sale process, those reverse mortgages would ultimately be a huge win for WSFS.

Nonetheless, the bank persisted in trying to find a buyer. Eventually, an institution in Wyomissing, Pennsylvania called Sovereign Bank began in-depth negotiations with Skip and Bill Abbott, the CFO of WSFS. Over the next couple of months, Skip and Jay Sidu, the CEO of Sovereign, would have several clandestine meetings in out-of-the-way hotels to discuss the possible transaction— trying to keep things under wraps until the deal was solidified. In December 1995, Sovereign made a nonbinding offer, subject to due diligence, to acquire WSFS at a price between $9.00 and 9.25 per share.

While this was a substantial premium over the then-market value of the company, the WSFS team considered it a lackluster, low-ball offer. At the beginning of the process, their collective analysis had indicated that the bank was worth somewhere between $9.00 and $14.00 per share; Given that the preliminary offer was at the bottom of the range, they felt negotiation was imperative. Skip and Jay went back and forth on the price, resulting in Sovereign's "final" offer of $ 9.25 per share.

The Future Begins

Early on the morning of March 4, 1996, the WSFS board met to consider Sovereign's ultimate proposal. All members were present and accounted for, plus the bank's advisors from Alex Brown & Co. and WSFS CFO Bill Abbott. A final offer on the table meant that hearty discussion would undoubtedly ensue. No matter what the outcome, it would be a consequential day for the Wilmington thrift.

Skip and Alex Brown recommended that the board reject the offer. Skip's argument did not come as a shock to board members: He had previously presented them with a nine-page analysis of alternative courses of action. This was his chance to articulate those points in person. While expressing the thought that the bid was not sufficient he also emphasized that remaining independent would require a lot of work and risk. WSFS would have to make some significant investments to build for the future. That would mean that in the short term, the bank would be less valuable until those investments bore fruit.[23]

"If we make this decision to remain independent, it is not a short-term decision," Skip told everyone. "Don't think we're going to take the bank off the market for six months and come back and market it again. If we follow the plan of investing for the future, we will be less valuable for a while. We must move ahead aggressively with plans for the future, or agree to remain as we are and be a caretaker organization while we wait to try to sell it again."

After significant discourse, there was a consensus that WSFS would accept the proposal if Sovereign increased the offer to $9.50 per share. With the two parties only $.25 apart, it was reasonable to expect that they'd find a way to settle.

Skip stepped out of the meeting to give Jay one last call. "Jay, you have to get to $9.50 or this deal is not going to move ahead," he said firmly.

But Jay wouldn't budge— he did not think that WSFS was worth an extra quarter. Somewhat bewildered, (but not completely disappointed), Skip returned to the boardroom to explain that negotiations had hit a wall.

In a surprising dramatic reversal from its earlier position, the board then voted unanimously not to sell the bank. It was time to move on— a huge sigh of relief for Skip, who felt like he had been vindicated.

With Time of Big-Buck Thrift Deals Past, Delaware's WSFS Decides Not to Sell

◆ By CHRISTOPHER RHOADS

The high multiples offered to thrifts last year are becoming a distant memory — a shift underscored last week by the decision of WSFS Financial Corp. of Delaware not to sell.

The $1.2 billion-asset Wilmington institution said that none of the expressions of interest it had received in recent months were much higher than its stock's recent trading price. As a result, the thrift will remain independent.

"It's sort of a sign of the times," said Arnold Danielson, president of Danielson Associates Inc., in Rockville, Md. "What it says is that the prices being offered for thrifts are not the high numbers we once saw, and that the big guys are not just throwing money around anymore."

WSFS' stock fell 69 cents to $8 in Nasdaq trading during the two days following the announcement last week. The stock had traded as high as $10 when the thrift announced last summer it had hired Alex. Brown & Sons Inc. to explore selling opportunities.

Marvin N. Schoenhals
Chief executive,
WSFS Financial Corp.

Officials and analysts said that the timing is probably not right for a sale for several reasons. For one, some of the usual acquirers in the area themselves have been bought, such as First Fidelity Bancorp of Newark, N.J. Others, such as First Union Corp. of Charlotte and CoreStates Financial Corp. of Philadelphia, are too busy digesting recent acquisitions.

Alex Hart, analyst at Ferris, Baker Watts Inc. in Baltimore, said the lack of a resolution from

Congress on the future of the Savings Association Insurance Fund has also cooled the thrift market at the moment.

"If it were my decision, I wouldn't walk into an unquantified liability," Mr. Hart said. "I really don't think that we will have much success with thrift acquisitions until the SAIF issue is resolved."

With buyers becoming pickier, thrifts wind up on the bottom of the list, particularly with their higher-cost deposits and mortgages, Mr. Danielson added.

WSFS officials said they are focusing now on long-range plans, but would still consider offers.

With 43% of the company's stock in the hands of the board, the directors have the shareholders' interests at heart, said Marvin N. Schoenhals, WSFS' chief executive.

"It was our assessment that our shareholders are best served by remaining independent," Mr. Schoenhals said. "We believe that the value of the company with its earning power is better than the indication of value received from potential acquirers."

165

"The Board of Wilmington Savings Fund Society announced this morning that it would remain independent, i.e., a sale agreement at a price attractive to the Board and Quad-C (as WSFS' largest shareholder) could not be reached," wrote Ted Wescler in a letter to Quad-C investors.

"Although we had hoped that the frothy bank acquisition market would result in a strong valuation and liquidity event for our WSFS stake, the market thought otherwise. We are fortunate to have a strong CEO, Skip Schoenhals, running WSFS as well as an institution whose risk profile has improved significantly since we invested in this situation a little over three years ago.

"For his part, Skip views the non-sale as a further catalyst for change at the bank and, in his words, 'feels energized to continue to push for cost reductions and growth in the Delaware franchise.'"

The Board's decision opened the gates to a new era for WSFS. The phoenix, now fully risen from the ashes, would soon learn to spread its wings and fly.

On that note, we conclude Book 1. Over the next few years those Seeds of Success discussed in Chapter 9 would bear much fruit. Skip, Mark and Karl Johnston would lead a team that built a foundation that undergirds WSFS to this day.

---

[23] One of the most significant investments would be the need to build a first-class business banking division. That would begin in earnest with the hiring of Karl Johnston in 1997. Karl and the team he assembled built it from the ground up, and his leadership paved the way for the division to become the dominant force that it is today. We will talk more about Karl in Book 2.

WSFS nearly was buried in 1990. But now, 'it's among the best-run thrifts in the country,' one analyst says.

WSFS Chairman and CEO Marvin "Skip" Schoenhals, in his office at 838 Market St., Wilmington, led the financial institution's remarkable turnaround. Schoenhals likes the idea of serving "small business customers who want access to their decision-maker."

CEO leads thrift from failing to phenomenal

By JONATHAN D. EPSTEIN
Staff reporter

Skip Schoenhals doesn't consider himself a betting man. But two years ago, he took what some might call a big gamble — and now he's happily watching it pay off.

In early 1996, with banks and thrifts nationwide being bought out at record prices, the chairman and chief executive of WSFS Financial Corp. led directors as they decided not to sell the thrift. After having solicited bids for eight months to explore their options, WSFS officials decided they could do better by going it alone.

Few shareholders are likely to begrudge the decision.

Since the beginning of 1995, WSFS stock has more than quadrupled, closing Friday at $20. More than half a dozen stock analysts are now highly recommending the company to investors, helping to jack up the price. And business overall is booming to boot, as officials look to expand their commercial lending presence in northern Delaware — and even open retail branches in nearby Pennsylvania.

Not bad for a thrift that seven years ago was on the verge of a catastrophic failure that would have wiped out the state's second-largest financial institution.

"Our performance has proven the wisdom of that decision to remain independent," said Schoenhals, who likes to say that WSFS stock has even outperformed Microsoft Corp. "There are very few institutions that had that magnitude of a turnaround."

Since coming to Wilmington from Michigan in November 1990, the Midwestern-bred Schoenhals — whose given name is Marvin but who prefers the nickname "Skip" — has reversed the ailing fortunes of the 165-year-old thrift. In the process, WSFS has not only recovered from its past struggles, but is being transformed into a viable commercial competitor for local banks.

In fact, WSFS doesn't even want to be thought of as a thrift anymore. Whereas a traditional thrift, or a savings institution, might have 80 percent of its loans in mortgages, only 25 percent of WSFS' portfolio is single-family residential loans.

Instead, WSFS wants to be a "high-performing" financial services institution, serving both households and small businesses, without abandoning its origins in mortgages.

"We want the world to know that we offer a full range of products," Schoenhals said.

And, he stressed, officials have no plans to disappear from the local landscape.

"My goal is to help make WSFS the kind of organization we've described and to retire from WSFS with it being one of the top-performing banks in the country," Schoenhals said. "I don't want to turn around and sell."

That makes the thrift's largest shareholder happy.

"Management's doing an excellent job. I'd just like them to continue the way they're doing," said John W. Rollins Sr., chairman and chief executive officer of Rollins Truck Leasing Corp., who owns about 14 percent of the stock. "You can't stand still. The only difference between a rut and a grave is they throw dirt over you in one."

Losses had soared to $90 million

In fact, WSFS almost was buried in 1990. That's when the mild-mannered Schoenhals was brought in under pressure from a powerful Philadelphia shareholder to try to save the thrift.

See WSFS — E6

Sidebar: Contributions to a World-Class Investor (Ted Weschler's Story)

These days, the investing world might know Ted Weschler for his role as portfolio manager at Berkshire Hathaway— with his office just a few steps away from the firm's legendary founder, Warren Buffett. But back in the early 90s, he was a fresh-faced Wharton graduate, learning the ropes of private equity with the guidance of his Quad-C co-founder, Terry Daniels.

While Ted's passion for the financial world would have propelled him towards success in the industry no matter what, there's one experience that he particularly credits with getting him to where he is today: his involvement in WSFS. His words here leave no questions as to how he felt about the historic old thrift and the people he got to learn from during his time on the board.

Born in Buffalo, New York in 1961, young Ted grew up in the Rust Belt, moving often because of his father's position as an executive of A&P— then the largest grocery retailer in the U.S. By the time he was six years old, he was an avid coin collector: a hobby that led to his active participation in the stock market at the ripe old age of 12.

In 1979, Ted enrolled in the University of Pennsylvania's Wharton undergraduate program. Besides gaining a firm grasp of the ins and outs of finance and accounting, Ted graduated from Wharton with something else that would prove significant to his life's journey: his friendship with Mark Schoeppner. While they were roommates for only a week, the two bonded over their Western Pennsylvania roots and love for all things stock market-related. So, when Mark introduced Ted to Skip in the summer of 1992, thinking that Quad-C might be interested in becoming a lead investor in WSFS, Ted was inclined to trust his friend's sharp instincts.

The rest, as they say, is history. What follows are some of Ted's thoughts about WSFS and its key players, collected from a series of recent interviews. His comments have been edited for length and clarity.

"Every year I do a couple sit downs with business school classes, and I frequently get the question of what experience do you think shaped you or what do you suggest for us developmentally? I think that the learning experience for me at the bank was like nothing else in my life.

You can get accounting and you can get finance out of textbooks. You can be a good analyst from doing the work. To be a really good investor, you need to know how people work, too. Obviously I'm biased, but my boss, Warren Buffett— I think he is the best alive. The more I work with him, the more I realize that what makes him tick is that he's got an uncanny sense of financials and finance and all the intricacies of accounting, but where he really shines is his understanding of behavioral finance.

My experience at WSFS and on the board there, that was my exposure to real-time behavioral finance. To understand what a group of people sitting around a table think about. There's a mindset on Wall Street, and particularly among people who manage money for a living, that they know the right things for corporations to do and they can't understand why those right things don't get done sometimes. But the fact of life is that boards are a group of people. They've got all those quirks that come with being a group of people. You've got subgroups within the board, you've got the dynamics of the people that work together, and sometimes the chemistry is great, sometimes it's not. Sometimes ideas take years to develop because you need to bring people along.

To have the benefit of Skip and CG and Gene Weaver and Tom Preston and Joe Julian... every one of them, very different from the other. Every one of them wanted to do the right thing. Every one of them took great pride in the institution. To be able to work shoulder to shoulder with these guys and work through the day-to-day of banking, but also to understand the 'people' dynamic and the tough decisions that have to be made— and how those decisions evolve in the committees and in the boardroom— it was just highly instructive to me. The education that came to me through the experience and the kindness and generosity of the folks I worked with there, you can't replace it.

Personally, the most significant learning experience of my lifetime was getting on that board and having these guys take me under their wing and educate me. They saw this 31-year-old and respected me for the things that I knew a little bit about, but also brought me along on things like credit analysis and company culture. Skip was particularly good on that stuff.

One of the toughest things in business is to retrofit a culture. It's one thing to start from a blank sheet of paper and imbue a business with what it needs. It's another thing to inherit something that's broken and then put the effort into making it work again and making it feel good about itself. Skip was clinical when he came in as the CEO. It was very hard to sell those southern branches. Very hard to let a lot of good, long-time people go. Very hard to monetize, terminate the pension and get some money out of that, but you have to do some tough stuff to make the patient survive. Then once you get through that, it becomes a building exercise. What can you do to go from 'can we survive' to 'can we flourish?'

Skip is unbelievably patient. Once in a while he would very politely tell me that I was crossing a line and micromanaging. I lived and breathed WSFS, but he'd say, 'This is actually not the sort of thing you should get involved in.'

He and CG and the board, they started this rebirth of the culture that took pride in the institution. That's one of those things that, again, you can't do with a decision, like shutting down the pension plan or raising high yield debt or what have you. It's something that is slow but steady. He did it in spades.

You look at the people that he brought in, and you look at the way he coached the people that he had. He always had a mindset of 'if there's a great person available, I'm going to get that great person in, and give people leeway to do their thing.'

I've been on a lot of boards since then, but what a rare mix it was to have this diversity of people. You had Skip at the reins, who was able to harness this diversity of thought, diversity of skills, and get everybody working together. That was both at the board level and at the bank. That's the sort of thing that creates greatness.

I wrote CG a note for his retirement party that he's the 'lead domino.' It's that example of somebody who does something that starts so many things down the road happening. Skip, CG, Mark Turner...for me to count all those guys as friends, it's pretty special.

Here's this institution that is, without question, the finest banking establishment in the state of Delaware. If you said 24 years ago that they were going to be meaningfully better than the legendary Wilmington Trust[24]— which had a 40% market share in Delaware at the time—I would have said impossible. Impossible.

From an investment standpoint, it basically turned into a 'hundred bagger' at Christmas of 2016. For every dollar put in in 1992, if you had held it that whole time and got the dividends, that dollar turned into 100 dollars. Whenever you get a hundred bagger in the world of investing, that's a big deal. It's exceptionally rare, and even rarer in the world of financial services. It's a legendary investment in my mind."

It's such a life lesson. With consistency, steadiness and patience, WSFS rose up against almost insurmountable odds."

---

[24] On November 1, 2010 Wilmington Trust announced that it would be acquired by M & T Bank of Buffalo, New York at a price $3.84 per share. This was 46% less than the closing price the day before. The sale was made necessary as a result of asset quality issues that arose from the financial crisis of 2007 - 2008.

A Speck of Dust— Reflections by Skip

This section of the book contains stories that should not be lost, but did not easily fit into the big narrative of WSFS' journey from Failing to Phenomenal.

How Did I Do It?

Over the years people have often asked me, "How did you lead WSFS through such a perilous time?" There are two answers to that question: One that deals with a broad perspective of the journey, and one that deals with a deeply personal perspective. Both are critical to my answer.

The **broad perspective** is pretty simple, yet encompasses many components.

WSFS had great bones when I arrived - By that, I mean the heritage of the company built in the prior 158 years. The customer loyalty was phenomenal, even throughout the period of ugly headlines. I am still amazed by the many stories I've heard about that fierce loyalty, but one in particular stands out. It was 1991: In the middle of what we now know was the depth of the crisis. I was talking with a customer who had nearly a million dollars in the bank. With the then-current FDIC insurance limits, that meant the majority of his funds were uninsured, so he would lose them if the bank did get closed. Despite that looming threat, he was steadfastly committed to keeping his money at WSFS. He said, "I am not withdrawing my money. With the history of this bank, it is not going away." While I was quite sure the bank would survive, I was frankly nervous about his decision, given all that I knew. But I stayed quiet, and he was right.

Another example of community attachment to WSFS: Hundreds of people have shared with me those quintessential early childhood experiences, when a parent or grandparent brought them into the mammoth lobby of our headquarters building at Ninth and Market Streets to open their first savings account. Many would recall how they had stared wide-eyed at the N.C Wyeth mural that occupied the entire south wall of that three-story lobby, and some would proudly tell me that they still had their first passbook.

A team of great people - Many were at the bank when I arrived, and many joined us along the way. I would love to start mentioning names, but there are so many that it would go on and on and I would likely leave some off. Suffice it to say that the success of WSFS was not a one-man show, but a beautiful tapestry of all of those individuals. Thank you to each of them. You know who you are.

Regulatory Courage. One of the most unappreciated aspects of the WSFS story is what I call "regulatory courage." Given the bank's condition in 1991, the easiest decision for the regulators would have been to close WSFS. While Delawareans would have bemoaned the loss, there would have been no serious condemnation of the regulators. The bank was so sick that one could easily say, "What choice was there?" The history of troubled banks would clearly indicate that closing WSFS was the right decision. In fact, at the end of 1990, there were nearly 400 thrifts with capital ratios at the WSFS level of .28%. Two years later, all but a handful had disappeared.

On the other hand, by giving us time to work, the regulators faced a huge risk. Had WSFS not made it, they would have been bombarded with one question: "What were you thinking?" But they took that risk, and thousands of us are really glad they did. Taxpayers should be grateful, too: that courage saved them several hundreds of millions of dollars. It's small potatoes in this new normal of a trillion here, a trillion there and oh, $5 trillion there, but closing WSFS would have cost the FDIC— and therefore, regular people— $200 million. And that's not counting the hundreds of millions that WSFS has since paid in income taxes.

As told in Chapter 7, I believe that Robert Gough was an important part of this courage, but it was not just him. Many people in both the OTS and the FDIC participated in the decision to give WSFS a chance to succeed.

Good Luck - I would love to say we did it all ourselves, but frankly we had some incredibly good luck on the journey. Things like the Fed maintaining a favorable interest rate environment that made it easier for bank earnings to recover; no economic downturn in the critical years; other small serendipitous events, too numerous to count, that happened at just the right moment.

And yes, thankfully, many good decisions along the way which fortunately outnumbered the bad ones.

A Speck of Dust

The **personal perspective** starts from the events in my life during the three years prior to joining WSFS in November 1990. In those three years, I had been fired twice and had my job eliminated once—meaning three separate periods of unemployment.

The first firing was completely unexpected and wounded me deeply, as it came 19 years into what up to then had been a successful, rapidly-advancing career. At that point, I was in the outer circle of the inner circle of a major bank holding company in Michigan. With the value of hindsight I can say that I understand the decision my boss made, but at the time it was devastating because it came out of the blue.

I did find another job in less than three months, but I was let go again only six months later— this time simply because the son of the bank's owner did not like me. The following half a year was spent looking for a job yet again: Ushering in a particularly demoralizing stretch of time where my wife and I had to face the fact that we might not be able to pay our bills. While being in that situation would be a terrible hardship for anybody, for a banker and former banker, it was an unthinkable reality. Thankfully, we made it through.

Eventually I landed a job as president of a bank in Michigan that had gotten itself into difficulty and needed a turnaround leader. Like WSFS, it was a pretty interesting journey, but never with the threat of closure. Once the bank was fixed, it was obvious that the best long-term solution was to sell it immediately. So we did, and the acquiring bank eliminated my position.

I tell all of this to set the stage for a late night in my office at WSFS in about February of 1991. Those periods of unemployment had not been easy for me. In fact, they had been so incredibly unpleasant, that for years afterwards I could not look at the 'Help Wanted' pages of the Wall Street Journal without a wince of deep emotion. During those three job searches, that section had been my lifeline because it was a major source of leads. The page would be updated once a week— I believe it was on Thursday— and on that day, I would open the paper with great anticipation that my perfect job would be there. As explained in Chapter 5, that hope did indeed come true one day with CG's little ad. However, by that point I was about nine months into the search; some 40 weeks of jumping to that page. Most of the time, the result was a big disappointment.

That section has long been gone, replaced by a whole new world of job posting on the internet. One might think that once I had found employment, the meaning those pages had for me would have diminished. Not so. While I stopped jumping to them, it took years for me to stop wincing whenever I was leafing through the paper and happened upon the job section.

On the particular evening I mentioned, I happened to be sitting in my office, reflecting on how bad the bank's situation was. That $37 million loss during the fourth quarter of 1990 had been much larger than I had anticipated— essentially wiping out all the bank's capital. As discussed, the bank was in a very deep hole. I had to acknowledge that there was a very low likelihood that WSFS would survive. If it did not, the FDIC would take over and send me packing immediately, sell the good parts of the bank and work out the bad parts.

As the high probability of that eventuality sunk in, I panicked. My thoughts swirled: Fired twice in less than a year, job eliminated 18 months later, and now president of a troubled bank that failed. Ouch. Those are pretty tough headlines to get behind during a job search. Sitting there, I envisioned never being able to get a position at a bank again, let alone the CEO spot. I was terrified. What could I do?

But then, God stepped in. He made me think about the fact that because of faith in Jesus, I have the absolute assurance of eternity with Him[25]. From that point of view, whether WSFS succeeded or failed, it was not even a speck of dust in the universe: It did not matter. Yes, failure would make my near-term life very challenging, but that would be a relatively short period when compared to eternity— where there are no tears, no sickness, no pain, just the Glory of God!

That change in perspective was huge. Why? Because if I hung on to the thought that my career was over if WSFS failed, I would have been anxious, worried, scared and weighed down by unhealthy thoughts as I came to work each day. If I had gotten caught in the idea that "I could not let WSFS fail," my anxiety would have translated into rotten performance. People that are deeply afraid of failure usually end up making mistakes because they are trying too hard. But because of the focus on eternity with God, I was able to come to work each day relaxed, determined to do the best that I could. Surprisingly, I would even usually get a good night's sleep.

That demeanor is more a part of how I "did it" than anything else.

The Value of a Quarter

One of the most fascinating untold stories of the WSFS journey surrounds two discussions that Ted Weschler and I had over the value of a quarter ($.25) in assessing the worth of a stock. The first instance is described in Chapter 10, when we were considering the potential sale of the WSFS to Sovereign Bancorp. In that case, our collective analysis was that the minimum sale price for WSFS would be $9.50 a share. Sovereign would not increase their offer from $9.25. While there were some that believed it was not worth losing the deal over $.25, Ted and I both said, "let it go." By now, you know the rest of the story— it was the right decision.

What would have happened if we had taken the Sovereign offer? In the 25 years from March of 1996 to March of 2021, the price of WSFS's stock appreciated 1,859%. Over the same period, the value of Sovereign's stock (including after it was acquired by Santander Bank in 2009) declined by 85%. Enough said. Both calculations exclude dividends.

Back in 1994, however, Ted and I had had another discussion about being $.25 apart in valuing a stock. As told in Chapter 9, when we were 'Sowing the Seeds' for the bank's future, we were also negotiating to acquire the San Francisco-based reverse mortgage lender, Providential Home Income Plan, Inc. The board had authorized Ted and I to settle the final terms of the transaction within a certain price range, and I had gone to Boston to discuss matters directly with the president of the hedge fund. Over the course of two days, all the particulars of the deal were worked out— except for price.

This time, their minimum price was $.25 higher than our maximum price. In contrast to the Sovereign story, I became convinced that in this case it was not worth losing the deal over a quarter. Ted was not there: His disciplined thinking caused him to say no to increasing in the offering price, sticking to our analysis. In a phone call where the two of us were trying to figure out what to do, I eventually said, "Ted, our projections for reverse mortgages show so much potential upside that if it's a good deal at $3.75 per share, it's still a good deal at $4.00— their minimum." His surprising response? You're right." Another great decision!

Leadership and Courage

When people talk about leadership, they often emphasize having a vision and getting others to become engaged in that vision. I certainly agree with that, but there is a side of leadership that is often overlooked: courage.

Leadership often demands difficult decisions that require courage to overcome one's emotions, the desires of others; to change the way things have 'always been done;' even to tell people, sometimes a lot of them, that they no longer have a job.

One of the most painful experiences at WSFS for me was when we sold the deposits of the 'downstate offices' to Wilmington Trust in 1991— part of the original capital plan explained in Chapter 7. Sometimes when branch offices are sold, the Associates (employees) go to the acquiring bank. But in this case, Wilmington Trust was folding the customer relationships into their own branch system, so they did not need any of the WSFS Associates. Therefore, approximately 50 WSFS Associates would lose their jobs with the sale. I felt it imperative that those 50 people hear the news— and the reasoning behind it— directly from me. So, the night before the announcement was to be made public, we invited all downstate Associates to come to the Dover office. Standing in front of them and saying, "I have sold you out of a job," was one of the most agonizing things I have ever done. My own memories of being unemployed were still fresh, so I identified deeply with the distress about to be inflicted.

Sure, I could have avoided that experience by asking someone else to deliver the message. In fact, Gordon Dyott, EVP in charge of Retail Banking at the time, volunteered to do it on my behalf. While he would have been sympathetic to those 50 people, he could have ducked the guilt part by saying it had not been his decision. Gordon would have never done that, but it would have still been easier for him.

Unfortunately, that would not be the only time I'd have to relay bad news to Associates. During those first two years, we had to reduce staffing by approximately 30% out of sheer necessity— translating to well over 100 people with their own hopes, dreams and families to support. As a business decision, it was absolutely essential: WSFS simply would not have survived otherwise. But on the human side of things, it was certainly something we wished we could have avoided.

Lest you think I always had courage, the answer is of course, no. Writing this book reminded me of some of those times. However, there is one situation that I remember with some degree of regularity even without writing the book. It happened in early 1991. That, of course, was a time of intense pressure to stay focused one thing: REDUCING PROBLEM ASSETS.

The bank had to publish the 1990 Annual Report by mid-March. Obviously we wanted to make it as simple and inexpensive as possible, i. e. no pictures and in black and white. The design people, however, thought it had to have a picture of the 'person in charge.' I said 'ok,' if it was a simple black and white photo. They arranged for me to go to a photographer's studio for a picture session. I was expecting a short, 'smile, click and be gone' session, but that was not what they had in mind.

They had set up for an elaborate photo shoot, complete with, "take your shirt off, it needs to be ironed." Note in the picture on the next page how neat the shirt looks. Well the session stretched to over three hours. I did not have time for that, but I did not want to embarrass anyone so I gritted my teeth and went through with it.

To this day I regret that after 15 minutes I did not say, "Enough! Take the picture and we are out of here." Maybe some would have been embarrassed, but my actions would have conveyed a very strong message—we have one focus and it is not a pretty picture! Besides, a rumpled shirt, rolled up sleeves and tie askew would have sent an important message as well. It is one of those stories that would have been repeated within the bank, "Can you believe he did that?" By doing so, the impact would have been magnified. I regret that my courage failed that day.

Earned Leadership versus Positional Leadership

I was in my mid-thirties, working at a bank in Owosso, Michigan. I was asked to fill a vacancy on the Owosso City Council. After the first year, I had to stand for election, and I won. Although the mayor was the official leader of the Council, as a result of my demeanor and doing my homework, I had emerged as the unofficial leader during those previous 12 months.

Under the city's charter, the mayor was elected by the Council after the Council had been elected by the citizens. This particular mayor had already served for years, so it was expected that he would run again. But he had a different idea. In what was an incredible act of courage and humility, he came to me prior to the citywide election and said, "Skip, through your actions and communications, you have become the real leader of the Council. If I run for another term, I will be re-elected, and the rest of the Council will feel obligated to re-elect me as the mayor."

He went on to say that it would be much better if I became the official leader of the Council— meaning he was going to drop out of the running altogether. In an unlikely turn of events, he had cleared the path for me to become the mayor of Owosso.

That episode taught me the value of earned leadership versus conveyed leadership. Leadership is earned when a person displays authentic qualities that make them worth following. Leadership is also conveyed by authoritative titles: like a general in the military. When he or she walks into a room, everybody immediately knows who has the power. While not necessarily a bad thing, relying on conveyed leadership will only go so far. A title can protect a poor leader for a finite amount of time, but a genuine leader who earns the respect of those around them becomes a great leader.

Culture

Many will debate whether it is better for an organization to have good strategies or a good culture. Ideally, it should be both. If you had to pick one, however, I firmly believe that 'culture eats strategy for breakfast.' Here are two examples of this philosophy at work.

Beginning in about 1995, WSFS began to focus on creating a 'Culture of Engagement.' In short, that involves or at least starts with two fundamentals: matching the 'wiring' of a person to the requirements of the job, and providing good supervisors.

Let me give you an example of the first. I am pretty sure that I am smart enough to pilot an airliner, but you would not want to be a passenger on a plane I was flying. Why? Because the way I am wired is not what is required to fly a plane (and that would be dangerous). No matter how many weeks of 'improvement training' I was given, I would never become a proficient— or safe— pilot. Since my wiring was not right to be a pilot, I would always be frustrated (to say nothing of the passengers). Give me a job suited to my wiring, and I become a much happier, engaged Associate. The next step is to ensure that every Associate has a first-class supervisor. While other things matter in building an awesome culture, get these two things right, and an organization is off to the races[26].

By the early 2000s, we had gotten this well established, and had the research to prove that our customers were receiving world class service. As a result, when I accompanied business banking Associates on customer development calls, as part of my 'sales pitch,' I could guarantee an extraordinary banking experience to the prospective customer. When they looked at me a bit quizzically, I could just point to the Gallup report on what our own customers said.

Do good products, or strategy, matter? Of course, but being able to truthfully say "We Stand for Service" matters more. That is a product of culture.

Culture also has factored into the dynamics of the WSFS Board of Directors and continues to do so to this day. Over the years the WSFS Board has been evaluated by many outside experts. In addition, many of our board members sit on other boards as well, and most of us have attended 'board best practices' seminars. In all these comparison points the result was always the same: the WSFS board comes out as 'the best.' Why? Simple answer: the Board Culture.

Years ago, the board created a vision of being a high performance board. That meant several things— like recruiting high-quality members, following (and creating) best practices and being very strategic. But the overall reason the board succeeded in its high-performance goal was culture. The board's key tenets were, and still are, as follows:

• It is committed to adding value to the organization.

• It holds itself accountable for its performance.

• Board members must have the courage to be independent and to raise controversial subjects, but must do so in a spirit of collegiality and respect for all.

• It recognizes that board members must vote their true convictions, and that unanimous votes are not required.

• It is committed to a diversity of inputs in decision-making (i.e. full discussion and consideration of all possible outcomes) but unity of support in implementation of decisions (i.e. no complaining to others about not agreeing with the decision, regardless of the outcome).

Miscellaneous Stories Worth Telling

When Skip's expectations were too low—Chapter 8 talked about the importance of John Rollins to the rights offering in 1992 that raised over $10 million of capital— a critical step in the path to becoming phenomenal. John had invested over $2 million in that effort (plus his original million-dollar investment). The day after the offering closed, I was in John's office with his wife Michele and his chief financial officer, Gene Weaver, who would later become a valued WSFS director. As one might imagine, John's office was quite expansive, on the top floor of what was then called the 'Rollins Building' on Route 202 in Fairfax (today it is The Wells Fargo Tower). The three of us were seated in front of John's massive desk, one of the largest I have seen. Off to the right was an equally-impressive conference table, adorned with some memorabilia. Among the assortment on the table was a model of the Gulf Stream jet that John owned.

At one point in the conversation, as only John could do, he made the comment that rarely, if ever, had he invested as much money as he had in WSFS when he "was not the majority stockholder." I am not sure what I said, but I was certainly appreciative that he had done so in the case of WSFS. Of course, I could read between the lines: He was also saying "don't screw up."

A few minutes later, John pointed out the Gulf Stream model. He commented that the one he owned was a Model 3 and that he was looking forward to trading up for Model 7.[27] I did not understand what that had to do with me, but then Gene made it clear. He said, "Skip, do you know what John is saying to you?" I had to admit

I was clueless. He said, "John expects his WSFS investment to pay for the new jet," Gene replied. I asked, "What would that cost?" "About $30 million."

My answer: "Guys, I am really optimistic about WSFS' future, but there is no way John's WSFS investment is going to grow that much, ever, let alone in the short term." I was wrong. Whether John ever upgraded his jet, I don't know, but the return on WSFS was such that it could have paid for the upgrade and then some. I'm glad they didn't take my word for it.

History Repeats Itself - To write Chapter 4, 'Banking in His Blood,' about CG's history, Brittany and I interviewed him a couple of times. I knew some of his story, but learned so much more as Brittany exercised her skill as a reporter. The most startling thing was hearing CG tell the story of walking into his dad's office and saying, 'Dad, I'm ready….so he made me President.' That scene was repeated many years later when Mark Turner, at the time EVP and Chief Operating Officer came into my office and said, "Skip, I am ready, it is time for me to become CEO." He used great logic, pointing to his extensive experience up to that moment in his career. In addition, he took the deep dive of pointing out that I had been promoted to my first bank CEO position at a younger age then he was at that time. Even though it was already well-settled that he would be my successor as CEO, he wanted to move then. As I recall, I did not set things in motion with the rapidity that it sounds like CG's dad did, but we worked it out.

A bad loan that became our home - One of the bad loans I discovered upon arrival did have a happy and enduring ending: It became our home at 500 Delaware Avenue. As additional security for another loan, the bank had placed a mortgage lien on a parking lot that comprised about one third of the block of Delaware Avenue between Washington and N. Jefferson Streets. When the original loan went bad, the bank foreclosed on the lot. Normally, a repossessed asset like that would have been sold immediately, but I thought it might be useful down the line. A few years later, WSFS acquired the remaining two thirds of the block and continued to operate the entire site as a parking lot. In 2007 owning that block enabled us to create the site for the WSFS Banking Center.

The Value of Good Partners

I said above that I would not start to mention names— there are just too many. But I conclude with acknowledging five incredible partners:

Charles 'CG' Cheleden   R. Ted Weschler   Mark Turner
Karl Johnston[28]   William Abbott

Each of these people played such an incredibly important role in the rising of this Phoenix, that I must conclude by saying WSFS would not be here without them.

THANK YOU GUYS!

Having recognized these five, I want to conclude with a tribute to the 'The First Domino,' Charles George Cheleden—better known as Charlie or really, to us only as CG. He started this journey to Phenomenal. I hope the importance of what he did and more importantly how he did what he did was clear to the reader. Most likely the most critical timing in this whole story was how quickly he was able to organize and complete the search for a new CEO. Because of the case study approach, I arrived with a plan. I did not have to figure it out after I got there, at least in a general way. Having the plan enabled us to hire PwC to do the asset review almost the day I officially became CEO. Hiring PwC gave me a valid reason to ask the OTS to delay the exam scheduled for November 1990. By the time the OTS came in February 1991, we had our problems clearly outlined. That gave them great confidence in the management team. Without the First Domino we would have been on the wrong side of the discussion. Would WSFS have been closed at that point, I don't know, but I do know it would have been much more likely.

25 The faith I'm referring to is a gift from God. It is a confident trust that the historical events of Jesus Christ's life, death, and resurrection have given me peace with God and the promise of victory over death. At a key point in my life, I came to realize that all of us human beings have fallen short of the goodness God requires of us, and in many cases we have done the opposite of what is good. What we deserve for this is eternal separation from Him (known as hell). But the good news for all of us is that through faith in the perfect life of the Son of God, Jesus Christ our Lord, His death on a cross, His resurrection from the grave and His ascension into heaven, we can have the assurance of peace with God starting now, and enduring forever. To trust in Jesus is the beginning of a relationship in which we leave behind our former path of living, and we begin down a new path of following him and becoming like him. It's not always an easy path, but it's a good path, and I wouldn't trade my life with Him for anything this world has to offer. If you would like to know more, I would encourage you to get a copy of the Bible in print or online and read The Gospel of Mark. It tells the story of who Jesus is and what he did for us. The next step would be to meet others who are on this new path with Jesus in a church near you. You can find a local church in your area here: https://www.thegospelcoalition.org/churches/. Feel free to reach out to me as well: Skip@mschoenhals.com

26 We plan to talk in greater detail about the WSFS Culture of Engagement in our next book. This quote from our Gallup partner tells a bit of the story, but doesn't tell how WSFS did it. That comes later. For now: "WSFS Bank was one of the early adopters of Gallup's Human Sigma science. In the course of its research, Gallup uncovered the special relationship developed between Engaged Associates and Engaged Customers, much greater than was previously known. In fact, just Engaging Associates produced a 70% lift in business results; just Engaged Customers also produced a 70% lift in business results, but when put together, Engaged Associates and Engaged Customers in the same relationship produced 240% lift in business results. WSFS embedded the principles and practices of both Associate and Customer Engagement, becoming a student and practitioner of the science. WSFS was selected as a Gallup Exceptional Workplace Award winner for five years and was also the recipient of the Culture Transformation Award."

27 I am not sure of the actual model numbers but the point is, he wanted to upgrade.

28 As noted earlier, Karl did not join WSFS until after the time covered by this book. Nevertheless, he was one of the incredibly important partners in this journey. I could not leave him off this list.

Appendix

Full articles from page 93 and 94.

New Star States CEO seeks Disney magic

By Peter Osborne, Staff Reporter

WILMINGTON—It's a bit disconcerting to hear a banker respond "Walt Disney" when asked to name a businessman who has influenced his career.

Until you hear Marvin N. "Skip" Schoenhals explain why.

"He created a vision no one else had and then went ahead and did it," says Schoenhals, a 43-year-old Michigan bank consultant who was named Wednesday as Star States Corp.'s new president and chief executive officer. "The company still operates under that vision long after his death. He brought together creative people and managed in such a way that he was able to please people and still bring an economic return to his stockholders."

In his new job as head of the parent company of Wilmington Savings Fund Society, Schoenhals (pronounced SHANE-HALLS) hopes to restore Disney-like magic to a kingdom that's seen better days. The soft-spoken banker confidently says he's up for what many believe is a formidable task.

"Star States has a rich heritage that impresses me," he says. "It was in a diversification mode that similar institutions got into in the mid-1980s and clearly made substantial mistakes."

"We must deal with the mistakes and go back to the heritage of being a class act. But it will require patience to work through the problems."

Schoenhals says it's too early to offer timetables—he wouldn't discuss the possibility of layoffs or whether Star States will sell B. Gary Scott Realtors—but cautions that those who expect the six-month turnaround he executed at his last job are likely to be disappointed.

"Problem assets don't go away overnight," he says. "We'll be trying to get our hands around the problems; the soft economy means it will take longer."

Schoenhals' appointment comes a little less than three months after Chairman and Chief Executive Officer J. Walton St. Clair Jr. and President Thomas K. Kerstetter announced their resignations on the heels of a $26.6 million second-quarter loss prompted by the write-off of a number of real estate investments and problem loans.

Although management said at the time that it was taking the big quarterly loss to "address its problems once and for all," Star States last week announced a $17.6 million loss spurred by more loan losses, a new $9 million provision for loan losses and some more ill-fated real estate development plans.

Star State's stock price over the last year has dropped from a high of $14.13 to about $2, where it's hovered for about a week.

Schoenhals says he's here for the duration, despite a resume that paints the picture of a turnaround specialist who leaves when the job is complete.

"My aspiration is not to be a wanderer," he says. "I want to deal with the short-term problems and then move on to build an organization that everyone is proud of.

"My job is to fix the problems and provide leadership. Doing that will create shareholder value. I'm not charged with getting the bank ready for sale. I hope we perform so well that our stockholders won't want to sell."

Michigan bankers who have followed Schoenhals' career say they'll believe that when they see it.

"He's a troubleshooter, and a good one," said one banker during last week's American Bankers Convention. "He engineered the sale of Peoples under fairly lucrative terms and it was a fiasco when he arrived. He's forthright and low-key, one of the most unbanklike people I've ever met."

Schoenhals left his job as president and chief executive officer of $380 million (assets) Peoples Savings Bank in Monroe, Mich., in January after it merged with the much larger Standard Federal Bank of Troy, Mich.

When Schoenhals arrived at Peoples in 1988, the bank was being investigated by the Federal Home Loan Bank Board for possible violations of securities laws. Shortly after going public, Peoples reported significant losses from problems in its consumer loan portfolio.

Within months, Schoenhals had restated the bank's financial statements for the previous three years, hired a new accounting firm, improved loan controls and replaced some personnel. The result? Delinquent loans were reduced by 75 percent to $1.5 million, charge-offs dropped 81 percent and net income jumped 60 percent to $2.4 million.

"Peoples' problems were about what I expected," Schoenhals says. "My charge was to fix the bank; no sale was contemplated. We ultimately looked at the bank's future and asked if we should consider a sale. We decided that if we were offered $18 per share, we probably had to let the shareholders vote."

Standard Federal paid $18.65 per share; when Schoenhals took over, the stock was selling for $8.

Schoenhals has spent his career eliminating problems. While some say "he gets rid of non-performing loans and non-performing people," Schoenhals prefers to say he's "an excellent leader who is hard on problems and works with people."

Thomas Cantalini, a Florida bank consultant who has been Schoenhals' chief financial officer in two turnaround situations, describes his former boss as "very methodical and thoughtful.

He lets you know what's expected but gives you time to do it. He's not the type to start letting people go (when he arrives), but he picks up pretty quickly who the performers and non-performers are."

Schoenhals' resume includes a 13-year stint with increasingly responsible positions at Grand Rapids, Mich.-based Old Kent Financial Corp., leaving the well-respected bank holding company as a senior vice president at its lead bank.

"As a manager, I guess I'm a blend between cheerleading and quiet leadership," he said. "All the cheerleading you do will fall on deaf ears if the substance isn't there. You can't be a chief executive officer and stay in your office all day. But I won't be someone who goes and parties with the staff, either."

Schoenhals says he can bring a new perspective to the problems at Star States. Discussion of corporate strategy mirrors what St. Clair and Kerstetter were saying until their departure: re-emphasize the core banking business and concentrate commercial lending on small businesses.

Of course, federal regulators have already dictated that approach. But those who know Schoenhals said the banker understands the juggling act necessary at Star States.

"He knows how to keep his eye on the ball," said attorney Eugene Driker of the Detroit law firm of Barris, Sott, Denn & Driker. "He knows how to keep the institution humming and still negotiate through the waves and bring the boat to shore.

"Many businessmen are linear thinkers—lining up the problems single file and then dealing with them. Not Skip. He understands the interrelationship between problems."

Says former Peoples Chairman Robert Scott: "His rapport with regulators is unbelievable..He's a straight-shooter."

He says he used to be a workaholic; now he's "an effective manager and leader (who) balances what he does."

Asked what he hopes others will say about him, Schoenhals paused before answering:

"That I am a fair and competent husband, father and manager. And that my relationship with God came first."

Full article from page 98.

$28 million loss rocks Star States WSFS parent concerned S&L may be in jeopardy

By Peter Osborne, Staff Reporter

WILMINGTON—The parent company of Wilmington Savings Fund Society said Friday it will lose up to $28 million in the fourth quarter and expressed concern over the thrift's ability to weather continued softness in local real estate markets.

Star States Corp. President Marvin N. Schoenhals said the thrift's future will be determined "over the next six to 12 months."

"We've identified our known problems," he said. "But if the real estate market gets a lot worse, we're going to have more problems."

The hefty fourth-quarter loss means Star States, which also owns B. Gary Scott Realtors, will lose between $70 million and $76 million - $14.58 to $15.83 per share—in 1990.

"I'm still convinced that this company will survive." Schoenhals said Friday afternoon. "We're concentrating on identifying all of our known problems and we've done that at this point.

"There is no indication that Star States is a target of the regulators. I believe [the federal Office of Thrift Supervision] is committed to working with the new management to allow [it] the opportunity to deal with the problems created by prior decisions."

Schoenhals said Star States will add between $12 million and $18 million to its loan-loss reserve, write down the value of intangible assets by $8.5 million, and settle a class-action lawsuit, paying $725,000 to stockholders who bought, sold or held Star States shares between Jan. 1, 1989, and July 17, 1990.

The sizable addition to the loan-loss reserve, which stood at $21 million in late October, came after a review of the thrift's loan portfolios and related assets by the Regulatory Advisory Services Group of the Price Waterhouse accounting firm.

Trading in the company's stock was halted for about 90 minutes before and after the midafternoon announcement. Trading resumed about 45 minutes before the market closed.

Star States closed at $1.875 per share, unchanged from Thursday's close.

Schoenhals was named president and chief executive officer of Star States and WSFS in November, three months after the resignations of Chairman and CEO J. Walton St. Clair Jr. and President Thomas K. Kerstetter amid disclosure of a $26.6 million second quarter loss.

Schoenhals said the cost-cutting measures being taken "are not likely to include across-the-board cuts in staffing or reductions in service levels. The subject of additional branch consolidations is under review."

Star States has filed an amended capital plan that lays out how it plans to meet increasingly harsh federal capital requirements. Schoenhals wouldn't discuss the particulars of the plan but predicted

Star States will shrink to about $1 billion in assets of the next few years. Those familiar with the company rate the thrift's future as a tossup between remaining independent. Merging with a large commercial bank or being taken over by regulators.

Under any of those scenarios, shareholder deposits up to $100,000 would continue to be insured by the Federal Deposit Insurance Corp.

Although it will hurt fourth-quarter earnings, devaluing the intangible assets will boost long-term profitability, Schoenhals and local brokers said. On Sep. 30, intangible assets totalled $16.1 million.

Star States has been evaluating the future economic benefits from the $10 million in goodwill resulting from its acquisition of Fidelity Federal Savings and Loan Association last February.

Goodwill—generally understood to represent the value of a respected business name or good customer relations—has no independent market or liquidation value and must be written off over a period of time, 15 years in this case.

Schoenhals conceded Friday that the acquisition "was not a good one for Star States," but quickly added that his assessment has the benefit of hindsight.

"We know a lot more today about Fidelity than we knew about them on the day of the acquisition," Schoenhals said. "Because of the growth restriction placed on us by regulators and the increasing deterioration in the real estate markets, what was a good loan then is not worth much today."

As a result of writing down the value of those assets, Star States will add between $700,000 and $1 million to its bottom line each year, beginning in 1991.

Schoenhals also said the thrift was not acknowledging its guilt in the shareholder suit but settled because "to defend the lawsuit would cost a lot of money and time" that could be better spent on other things.

The company's largest shareholder, Wilmington entrepreneur John Rollins Sr., said that while he hopes the problems are worked out, he's not responsible for the company's increasingly aggressive posture toward addressing the problems in its real estate portfolio.

"We're not going to sweep our problems under the table," Schoenhals said. "Here's the dirty laundry; now we're going ahead."

Full article from page 99.

WSFS not closing, regulator says

Flood of phone calls prompts comment

By Peter Osborne, Staff Reporter

WILMINGTON—A high-ranking federal regulator on Tuesday broke a long-standing policy against commenting on individual thrifts by describing as "absolutely baseless" rumors that Wilmington Savings Fund Society soon will be shut down by regulators.

In the past week, nearly $10 million in insured deposits have been withdrawn by nervous customers.

"WSFS is not being closed down and is not on any list to be closed down," said William C. Eayre, assistant director of the Office of Thrift Supervision's Pittsburgh office.

The comment is unusual in that it runs counter to a long-standing OTS policy against commenting on specific institutions under regulatory supervision. But a flood of customer questions to the thrift, regulators and media in recent days led regulators and WSFS management to fight back Tuesday.

Eayre said that while the troubled thrift is not yet out of the woods, it is taking steps to work out its problems. He added that while no regulator will make predictions about future actions, rumors of an impending closing are untrue.

"We normally don't comment on where individual institutions stand, but this is an absolutely baseless rumor," Eayre said. "We've been getting lots of phone calls from concerned customers. Whoever is starting these rumors is just flat wrong and is creating a lot of mischief and a lot of heartache."

Marvin N. Schoenhals, president and chief executive officer of WSFS parent Star States Corp., said the thrift received more than 100 phone calls from concerned customers asking about the rumors. But he said he was especially disturbed that some customers cashed in their certificates of deposit early, paying an interest penalty.

The nearly $10 million in deposits withdrawn from customer accounts represents less than 1 percent of WSFS's deposit base. Schoenhals said the withdrawals are coming from accounts that are covered by the Federal Deposit Insurance Corp.

Schoenhals said he was offering an amnesty program to depositors who were misled by the rumor mill.

"It's frustrating to me to see people sacrificing their money in this way," Schoenhals said. "We'll refund the interest penalty and reinstate the original rates to anyone who redeposits those CDs by the close of business next Tuesday."

Full Article from page 100.

Star States posts $37 million loss

By Peter Osborne, Staff Reporter

WILMINGTON - The housecleaning at Star States Corp. is under way in earnest.

The parent company of Wilmington Savings Fund Society and B. Gary Scott Realtors on Friday reported a $37.7 million loss for the fourth quarter, completing a dismal year that included setting aside $33.3 million for potential and actual loan losses.

The company reported a loss of $85.5 million, or $18.01 a share, for the year.

Star States also said it would lease its Star States Tower site property on Rodney Square to Wilmington developer Ernest F. Delle Donne, and had completed the sale of its Anderson Leasing subsidiary and other real estate assets.

President and Chief Executive Officer Marvin N. Schoenhals said the actions, combined with future asset sales, should allow the company to be profitable this year, unless the economy continues its tailspin.

"We believe all the problems are on the table; the unknowns are the economy and how our customers react," said Schoenhals, adding that he is continuing to focus on strengthening the company's core retail banking business.

The results announced Friday will come as little surprise to investors and customers since Star States management has been openly discussing its problems and even predicted a large loss in late December.

Star States stock closed Friday at 2 ⅛, up ¼. The loss was reported in mid-afternoon.

The $16.2 million addition to loan loss reserves in the fourth quarter, along with the goodwill writedowns, came after a review of the thrift's loan portfolios and related assets by the Regulatory Advisory Group of the Price Waterhouse accounting firm.

Although Star States had predicted it would lose up to $28 million in the fourth quarter, the additional loss was primarily due to devaluing its intangible assets by $5.7 million more than it planned in December.

Better known as goodwill, intangible assets—generally understood to represent the value of a respected business name or good customer relations—have no independent market or liquidation value and must be written off over a period of time. 15 years in this case.

With its decision to write down the $15.3 million in goodwill and assets accounting for more than 40 percent of the fourth quarter loss, Star States has now completely eliminated its goodwill.

Schoenhals said 1991 will be spent continuing the restructuring of operations. The primary subsidiary, WSFS, falls far short of complying with all three federal capital requirements.

Schoenhals said one way of improving capital is through the sale of assets, but did not elaborate beyond saying Star States would sell a 58,000 square foot site at 10th and Jefferson Streets in downtown Wilmington to Delle Donne.

He also said Star States has entered into "an agreement in principle" to consolidate WSFS operations into a single 60,000 to 80,000 square foot downtown site in 1992. He declined to say where that consolidation would take place but said the company's operations center on Philadelphia Pike would not be affected.

Federal regulators, to combat persistent rumors, recently took the unusual step of saying they had not targeted WSFS for closure.

www.ingramcontent.com/pod-product-compliance
Lightning Source LLC
Chambersburg PA
CBHW040852210326
41597CB00029B/4822